Index

to

Sussex County

Delaware

Wills

1800-1851

Marguerite R. Moore

HERITAGE BOOKS
2011

HERITAGE BOOKS
AN IMPRINT OF HERITAGE BOOKS, INC.

Books, CDs, and more—Worldwide

For our listing of thousands of titles see our website
at
www.HeritageBooks.com

Published 2011 by
HERITAGE BOOKS, INC.
Publishing Division
100 Railroad Ave. #104
Westminster, Maryland 21157

Originally published 1995
Family Line Publications

Other Heritage Books by Marguerite R. Moore:

Sussex County, Delaware Will Book L: 1 January 1852–24 February 1860

Sussex County, Delaware Will Book M: 8 March 1860–13 April 1869

International Standard Book Numbers
Paperbound: 978-1-58549-308-1
Clothbound: 978-0-7884-8670-8

INTRODUCTION

This volume contains an index to the testators whose wills were proved between the years 1800 and 1851. The index contains the full name of the testator, the dates the will was signed and proven, and the book and page numbers where the book can be found.

Persons desiring copies of a will may write to the State of Delaware, Division of Cultural and Historic Affairs, Hall of Records, Dover, Delaware, 19901.

Persons working on families from Sussex County, Delaware, are ask to contact the author, Marguerite Moore, 7730 Emerson Avenue, Los Angeles, CA 90045-1117.

Robert Barnes

NAME		WILL	PROBATE	BOOK	PAGE
ABBOTT	Easter	10 NOV 1844	8 JAN 1845	K	65
ABBOTT	James	10 NOV 1835	16 FEB 1836	H	316
ABBOTT	William	8 JAN 1842	11 FEB 1842	I	317
ABBOTT	William	17 NOV 1842	17 APR 1844	K	32
ADAMS	Ennals	18 OCT 1806	27 OCT 1812	F	507
ADAMS	Henry	26 MAR 1821	13 MAY 1828	H	16
ADAMS	Jacob	3 FEB 1809	17 NOV 1819	G	161
ADAMS	James	23 APR 1804	14 OCT 1807	F	302
ADAMS	John	21 SEP 1807	14 OCT 1807	F	299
ADAMS	Peggy	11 JUL 1807	9 MAR 1808	F	330
ADAMS	Roger	5 DEC 1806	15 MAY 1810	F	402
ADAMS	Thomas	18 FEB 1846	6 APR 1846	K	158
ADKINS	David	8 APR 1824	3 AUG 1824	G	340
ALEXANDER	William	29 MAY 1806	29 MAY 1806	F	231
ANDERSON	John	24 JUN 1812	30 JUN 1812	F	515
ARGO	Alexander	4 APR 1831	30 JAN 1832	H	152
ARGO	Andrew	14 OCT 1827	6 NOV 1827	H	6
ARGO	Isaac	1 AUG 1805	20 AUG 1805	F	198
ARGO	Jordon	1 JAN 1835	10 FEB 1835	H	276
ARGO	Joseph	28 NOV 18--	30 JAN 1819	G	181
ARGOE	Alexander	24 SEP 1820	7 OCT 1820	G	174
ARNEL	William	25 NOV 1842	18 APR 1849	K	383
ART	Bailey	10 JUN 1826	11 SEP 1826	G	437
ATKINS	Hannah	3 OCT 1799	12 NOV 1800	F	41
ATKINS	Margaret	1 AUG 1845	29 AUG 1845	K	109
ATKINS	Sary	6 JAN 1832	10 JAN 1832	H	146
ATKINS	Thomas	19 JAN 1832	31 JAN 1832	H	153
AYDELOTT	George	15 MAY 1803	9 APR 1804	F	379
AYDELOTT	Isaac	10 APR 1804	4 JUN 1804	F	142
AYDELOTT	Matthias	15 MAY 1801	13 JUN 1801	F	77
AYDELOTTE	John	10 JUL 1836	13 JAN 1837	I	19
AYDELOTTE	Matthias	16 APR 1801	9 JUN 1801	F	59
BAGWELL	Patience	19 JAN 1813	13 JAN 1820	G	162
BAILEY	Betsey	19 FEB 1814	8 MAR 1814	G	37
BAILEY	Davis	26 JUL 1806	4 OCT 1808	F	520
BAILEY	Louder	16 FEB 1814	8 MAR 1814	G	33
BAILEY	Samuel	26 MAR 1803	24 SEP 1813	F	526
BAILEY	Samuel	14 FEB 1814	22 DEC 1815	G	51
BAILEY	William	27 DEC 1834	15 JAN 1840	I	212
BAKER	Daniel	21 MAR 1810	23 JUN 1812	F	502
BAKER	Eunice	21 JUL 1840	28 SEP 1840	I	230
BAKER	Hester	14 JUN 1845	6 APR 1846	K	160
BAKER	Isaac	27 FEB 1823	13 MAR 1823	G	282
BAKER	James	27 OCT 1808	31 JAN 1817	G	91
BAKER	John	6 NOV 1808	28 NOV 1808	F	357
BAKER	Riley	16 JUN 1807	20 OCT 1807	F	298
BAKER	William	2 JUL 1849	14 MAR 1850	K	461
BALDING	Sarah	23 DEC 1799	8 FEB 1803	F	98

1

BALL	Levin	9 DEC 1818	29 JAN 1819	G	136
BANKS	Jacob	11 AUG 1805	7 JUL 1807	F	286
BANNING	Deborah	18 DEC 1838	24 DEC 1838	I	161
BARKER	Bagwell	8 FEB 1824	15 MAR 1824	G	321
BARNET	Lydda	14 SEP 1825	30 MAY 1826	G	425
BARTLET	Thomas	18 FEB 1805	21 MAR 1805	F	185
BARWICK	John	FEB 1850	19 MAR 1850	K	463
BEACH	Thomas	28 NOV 1825	14 DEC 1825	G	404
BEACH	Winder	5 JUL 1831	20 OCT 1838	I	149
BEACHAM	Charles	1 FEB 1844	12 MAY 1845	K	100
BEAUCHAMP	Isaac	25 JAN 1805	26 JAN 1805	F	179
BEAUCHAMP	Mary	12 DEC 1807	1 JAN 1808	F	316
BELL	Boaz	10 JAN 1837	11 FEB 1837	I	29
BELL	George	28 AUG 1841	30 SEP 1841	I	283
BELL	Henry	21 MAR 1829	12 NOV 1829	H	60
BELL	John	26 NOV 1812	12 FEB 1813	F	496
BELL	Nathaniel	9 JUN 1798	5 AUG 1803	F	100
BELL	Thomas	26 FEB 1849	20 AUG 1851	K	546
BELL	William	26 MAY 1796	30 OCT 1800	E	270
BENNETT	John	15 MAY 1815	16 FEB 1816	G	73
BENNETT	Joshua	11 NOV 1801	18 JAN 1802	F	74
BENNETT	Nehemiah	30 NOV 1811	7 JAN 1812	F	479
BENNEWELL	Soverign	10 JAN 1816	7 MAY 1821	G	207
BENNUM	George	31 DEC 1836	15 AUG 1838	I	140
BENNUM	Henry	16 NOV 1831	7 JUL 1841	I	273
BENSON	Jane	31 JAN 1841	18 MAR 1842	I	325
BETTS	John	20 FEB 1807	23 MAR 1807	F	278
BLACK	George	FEB 1826	5 FEB 1826	G	417
BLACK	John	6 NOV 1836	30 NOV 1836	I	12
BLADES	Greensbury	17 JUL 1838	15 SEP 1838	I	144
BLIZZARD	Loda	6 SEP 1851	7 OCT 1851	K	561
BLIZZARD	Stephen	30 MAR 1850	12 DEC 1851	K	575
BLIZZARD	Thomas	10 NOV 1828	13 JUL 1830	H	86
BLOODWORTH	William	9 MAR 1802	2 APR 1802	F	32
BLOXAM	John	16 NOV 1822	24 AUG 1824	G	343
BLOXAM	Richard	7 SEP 1806	21 MAY 1822	G	253
BLOXSOM	Aaron	1 MAY 1831	16 NOV 1831	H	137
BOLING	Luraney	3 FEB 1844	23 SEP 1844	K	40
BOLING	Thomas	27 JAN 1825	24 MAR 1825	G	383
BONNAWELL	Letty	5 OCT 1834	13 NOV 1834	H	266
BOSTON	Soloman	25 JUN 1819	19 JUL 1819	G	153
BOSTON	Solomon	2 APR 1848	21 APR 1848	K	278
BOWMAN	John	10 FEB 1818	8 DEC 1818	G	126
BOYCE	Asa	25 MAR 1817	28 MAR 1817	G	90
BOYCE	Hosea	7 SEP 1840	22 DEC 1840	I	249
BOYCE	Robert	10 APR 1837	20 MAR 1838	I	114
BOYCE	William	15 APR 1817	5 FEB 1818	G	122
BOYD	Adah	14 NOV 1795	7 OCT 1807	F	297
BOZMAN	Mary	18 MAY 1831	31 JAN 1832	H	

BOZMAN	Philemon	10 OCT 1833	4 FEB 1834	H	229
BRADLEY	Cannon	13 OCT 1800	6 JAN 1801	E	271
BRADLEY	Gedion	20 NOV 1800	3 DEC 1800	F	11
BRADLEY	Henry	25 JUL 1806	7 OCT 1806	F	242
BRADLEY	Isaac	20 SEP 1842	19 OCT 1843	K	8
BRADLEY	Joseph	18 SEP 1848	14 MAR 1849	K	353
BRADLEY	Joshua	3 NOV 1817	18 NOV 1817	G	99
BRADLEY	Josiah	9 OCT 1847	4 JAN 1848	K	262
BRADLEY	William	27 MAY 1812	25 NOV 1814	G	26
BRADLEY	William	12 JAN 1841	4 MAY 1841	I	267
BREDLE	Elihu	29 NOV 1822	18 JAN 1823	G	276
BRERETON	John	18 APR 1843	12 AUG 1843	I	395
BRERETON	Thomas	6 DEC 1819	28 DEC 1820	G	194
BROWN	Charles	20 APR 1806	24 JUN 1806	F	234
BROWN	Francis	28 MAY 1829	4 AUG 1829	H	47
BROWN	John	8 OCT 1804	9 FEB 1808	F	314
BROWN	John	1 MAY 1812	9 JUL 1812	F	491
BROWN	Martha	19 JAN 1820	22 FEB 1820	G	164
BROWN	Sarah	8 JUN 1831	13 MAR 1839	I	173
BROWN	Sinah	30 NOV 1850	25 JUN 1851	K	538
BROWN	Sophia	14 DEC 1818	23 MAR 1819	G	140
BRYAN	Mary	20 JUL 1811	22 FEB 1820	G	183
BRYAN	Nancy	20 DEC 1812	16 FEB 1813	G	3
BUNTIN	John	17 JUL 1813	12 OCT 1813	G	10
BURBBAGE	John	31 MAR 1847	2 APR 1847	K	228
BURBBAGGE	John	10 MAY 1835	9 APR 1840	I	222
BURTON	Aron	10 MAR 1798	15 MAR 1803	F	15
BURTON	Benjamin	2 JUN 1824	22 JUN 1824	G	322
BURTON	Coard	10 SEP 1842	11 OCT 1842	I	347
BURTON	Cornelia	27 MAR 1838	19 NOV 1846	K	202
BURTON	Daniel	3 JUN 1809	9 JUL 1809	F	400
BURTON	Daniel	7 APR 1822	9 MAY 1822	G	247
BURTON	Elizabeth	11 FEB 1841	23 FEB 1841	I	257
BURTON	Esther	28 FEB 1805	6 MAR 1805	F	182
BURTON	Jacob	19 NOV 1809	12 JAN 1810	F	378
BURTON	James	29 JUN 1823	9 FEB 1824	G	318
BURTON	Jeremiah	6 MAR 1811	13 MAR 1811	F	448
BURTON	John	29 MAR 1830	21 APR 1830	H	79
BURTON	John	9 JAN 1840	10 MAR 1840	I	218
BURTON	Joseph	14 JUN 1804	4 JUL 1809	F	417
BURTON	Luke	29 MAY 1810	31 JUL 1810	F	414
BURTON	Molly	25 OCT 1803	14 NOV 1803	F	124
BURTON	Rachel	8 OCT 1801	20 APR 1802	F	27
BURTON	Robert	7 JUN 1849	22 JUN 1849	K	396
BURTON	Samuel	2 APR 1823	17 JUN 1823	G	291
BURTON	Sophia	4 JAN 1820	12 FEB 1822	G	240
BURTON	William	6 JUN 1843	23 NOV 1843	K	19
BURTON	Woolsey	27 SEP 1800	20 APR 1803	F	94
BUTLER	Elizabeth	7 OCT 1803	13 AUG 1804	F	156

3

BUTLER	John	20 OCT 1817	5 NOV 1817	G	109
BUTLER	Samuel	17 DEC 1800	11 MAY 1802	F	45
BUTLER	William	31 JAN 1804	14 MAR 1806	F	223
CADE	Priscilla	21 MAR 1805	17 OCT 1811	F	470
CALHOON	Christopher	15 JAN 1834	3 FEB 1834	H	226
CALLAWAY	Ann	24 OCT 1807	19 AUG 1814	G	30
CALLAWAY	Benjamin	3 JUN 1814	10 JUN 1814	G	25
CALLAWAY	Clement	8 SEP 1814	23 DEC 1814	G	24
CALLAWAY	Isaac	24 MAY 1834	22 SEP 1835	H	299
CALLAWAY	Nehemiah	15 MAR 1815	8 SEP 1820	G	170
CALLAWAY	Wingate	24 JUL 1841	30 AUG 1841	I	278
CAMPBELL	John	4 APR 1810	31 MAR 1812	F	493
CAMPBELL	Nancy	2 JAN 1802	17 NOV 1802	F	7
CANNON	Amsolum	15 APR 1829	21 APR 1829	H	40
CANNON	Arcada	DEC 1815	8 FEB 1816	G	65
CANNON	Betty	6 FEB 1815	1828	H	21
CANNON	Ebenezer	22 APR 1816	10 MAY 1816	G	70
CANNON	Elisha	25 DEC 1810	5 JAN 1811	F	446
CANNON	Esther	17 SEP 1816	10 MAY 1819	G	143
CANNON	Ezekial	5 AUG 1833	4 SEP 1838	I	142
CANNON	Henry	22 MAY 1834	14 AUG 1834	H	251
CANNON	Hodson	23 DEC 1802	4 JAN 1803	F	67
CANNON	Hughett	12 DEC 1808	14 MAR 1809	F	367
CANNON	Isaac	5 MAY 1843	25 MAY 1843	I	388
CANNON	Jacob	18 JAN 1832	20 MAY 1833	H	201
CANNON	Jacob	12 JAN 1843	27 APR 1843	I	380
CANNON	James	19 DEC 1814	20 JAN 1815	G	39
CANNON	Joseph	5 DEC 1800	25 JAN 1803	E	315
CANNON	Joseph	20 NOV 1799	24 NOV 1799	F	446
CANNON	Joseph	18 NOV 1825	1825	G	402
CANNON	Joseph	1 OCT 1845	28 OCT 1845	K	124
CANNON	Josiah	10 AUG 1843	19 SEP 1843	I	399
CANNON	Levi	20 NOV 1837	17 JUL 1838	I	134
CANNON	Levin	25 FEB 1839	12 MAR 1839	I	171
CANNON	Mary	2 SEP 1816	13 SEP 1816	G	184
CANNON	Nutter	7 OCT 1841	15 OCT 1841	I	291
CANNON	Polly	3 MAY 1832	18 DEC 1832	H	184
CANNON	Sally	9 NOV 1809	27 AUG 1811	F	465
CANNON	Stephen	12 SEP 1798	17 JAN 1805	F	177
CANNON	Wingate	27 FEB 1850	5 MAR 1850	K	459
CAREY	Comfort	7 JUN 1817	21 JUN 1817	G	107
CAREY	Eli	16 JAN 1827	6 FEB 1827	G	446
CAREY	John	22 JAN 1832	14 FEB 1832	H	156
CAREY	Stockley	4 MAR 1809	22 JAN 1811	F	437
CAREY	William	8 JAN 1848	16 FEB 1848	K	266
CARLISLE	John	27 FEB 1809	21 NOV 1810	F	426
CARLISLE	Manlove	No Date	1 DEC 1815	G	51
CARLISLE	Pemberton	2 AUG 1810	13 NOV 1818	G	132
CARLISLE	Rachel	17 JAN 1833	24 SEP 1835	H	300

CARMEAN	Louder	21 APR 1841	4 MAY 1842	I	330
CARMEAN	Mary	19 MAY 1827	31 JUL 1827	G	455
CARMEAN	Milley	19 FEB 1818	11 FEB 1820	G	165
CARMEAN	William	9 FEB 1843	18 SEP 1844	K	47
CARNEL	Sarah	27 JUL 1822	10 MAY 1823	G	287
CARPENTER	Alice	3 OCT 1824	26 OCT 1824	G	357
CARPENTER	Hannah	10 JUN 1842	18 MAR 1845	K	88
CARPENTER	Jacob	4 DEC 1803	7 FEB 1804	F	143
CARPENTER	Jesse	27 SEP 1824	24 MAY 1825	G	388
CARPENTER	Laben	18 SEP 1823	21 MAY 1834	H	244
CARPENTER	Mary	7 MAR 1806	18 MAR 1806	F	220
CARPENTER	William	20 MAY 1799	19 MAY 1802	F	89
CARY	Charles	27 MAR 1812	23 SEP 1822	G	266
CARY	Elon	27 OCT 1799	15 OCT 1800	E	279
CHIPMAN	John	7 AUG 1826	9 MAY 1829	H	41
CLANDANIEL	John	16 NOV 1790	2 JAN 1801	E	268
CLARK	Jacob	22 JAN 1824	1 MAR 1824	G	320
CLARK	Rhoda	26 AUG 1829	6 JUL 1830	H	84
CLARK	Richard	12 MAR 1821	17 APR 1821	G	202
CLENDANIEL	Ahab	8 OCT 1800	16 APR 1805	F	188
CLENDANIEL	Areny	1826	26 SEP 1826	G	438
CLIFTON	Luranea	24 MAR 1808	19 APR 1808	F	334
CLIFTON	Mary	14 MAR 1817	15 MAR 1819	G	137
CLIFTON	Pemberton	9 JUN 1838	17 NOV 1842	I	360
CLOWES	Peter	25 SEP 1807	9 OCT 1811	F	467
COARD	Sally	2 AUG 1834	15 JAN 1845	K	66
COFFIN	Cornelius	9 MAR 18__	1 SEP 1829	H	50
COFFIN	William	19 JUL 1807	31 MAR 1807	F	273
COLBOURN	Kendal	24 AUG 1830	22 SEP 1830	H	92
COLLINS	Anthony	25 FEB 1811	10 APR 1811	F	456
COLLINS	Charles	4 DEC 1850	30 DEC 1850	K	503
COLLINS	Comfort	20 JAN 1801	1 NOV 1826	G	442
COLLINS	Curtis	13 NOV 1804	29 NOV 1804	F	171
COLLINS	Horatia	30 JUN 1834	13 NOV 1834	H	264
COLLINS	John	17 FEB 1804	12 MAR 1804	F	129
COLLINS	John	19 MAR 1814	14 OCT 1815	G	52
COLLINS	John	26 JAN 1821	21 FEB 1823	G	277
COLLINS	John	17 JAN 1827	MAY 1827	G	453
COLLINS	Joseph	10 APR 1822	15 MAY 1822	G	250
COLLINS	Lambertson	30 JUL 1847	17 FEB 1848	K	268
COLLINS	Levi	27 SEP 1850	14 FEB 1851	K	507
COLLINS	Polly	4 FEB 1816	23 MAR 1816	G	67
COLLINS	Rachel	11 NOV 1807	1 JAN 1808	F	309
COLLINS	Sally	10 SEP 1836	5 APR 1837	I	51
COLLINS	Sarah	16 SEP 1835	8 MAR 1844	K	30
COLLINS	Stephen	10 MAR 1849	28 AUG 1849	K	412
COLLINS	Thomas	25 SEP 1802	24 AUG 1811	F	471
CONNAWAY	John	29 JAN 1833	21 OCT 1846	K	196
CONNAWAY	Levina	6 OCT 1830	22 DEC 1832	H	185

5

CONWELL	John	21 AUG 1811	16 SEP 1811	F	465
CONWELL	John	1 SEP 1838	28 SEP 1838	I	146
CONWELL	William	8 OCT 1820	20 FEB 1821	G	200
CONWELL	William	21 NOV 1828	25 JAN 1831	H	98
COOK	Mary	24 JUL 1813	25 APR 1814	G	48
COOPER	William	1 AUG 1835	22 MAY 1849	K	390
COPES	Joseph	22 MAR 1820	23 APR 1822	G	245
CORD	Betty	25 SEP 1832	10 OCT 1837	I	70
CORD	Jane	4 JUN 1816	17 DEC 1816	G	86
CORDREY	John	17 JUL 1816	2 JAN 1821	G	194
CORDRY	William	3 AUG 1833	30 AUG 1833	H	208
CORNWELL	Avery	16 JAN 1835	5 FEB 1835	H	275
COULBORN	Thomas	10 SEP 1818	6 MAR 1821	G	201
COULBOURN	Catherine	16 JUN 1831	19 JUL 1831	H	122
COULBOURN	William	5 AUG 1837	3 OCT 1837	I	72
COULTER	Andrew	6 MAR 1793	11 APR 1803	F	34
COULTER	James	1 FEB 1808	21 JUN 1808	F	336
COULTER	Unice	18 APR 1803	17 JUL 1804	F	152
COUSTON	Ahab	12 JUL 1803	19 AUG 1803	F	105
COVERDALE	Levin	16 AUG 1801	26 AUG 1801	E	300
COVERDILL	Rachel	8 AUG 1800	7 OCT 1800	E	266
COVERDILL	Richard	16 DEC 1809	27 FEB 1810	F	405
CRAFFORD	George	14 NOV 1810	1 DEC 1810	F	428
CROUCH	William	25 NOV 1804	8 JAN 1805	F	190
CULLENS	John	26 JUN 1817	5 SEP 1826	G	436
CULVER	Moses	25 DEC 1813	22 JUL 1814	G	34
CURREY	Thomas	2 AUG 1827	6 NOV 1827	H	5
CURRY	Elizabeth	4 JAN 1829	23 JAN 1829	H	31
CURRY	Thomas	9 FEB 1836	10 MAR 1836	H	317
CURRY	Wingate	11 1829	25 FEB 1829	H	36
DALE	James	15 SEP 1812	2 AUG 1814	G	18
DANIEL	William	20 MAR 1804	26 APR 1804	F	125
DARHAM	Richard	No Date	20 SEP 1804	F	166
DARTERS	Hudson	5 JUL 1834	4 NOV 1839	I	206
DASHIELL	Winder	2 MAR 1850	11 JUN 1851	K	531
DAVENPORT	Mary	24 NOV 1818	28 NOV 1818	G	130
DAVIS	John	13 JAN 1832	17 JAN 1832	H	146
DAVIS	Mark	23 FEB 1839	2 APR 1839	I	175
DAVIS	Mary	7 JUL 1810	6 NOV 1810	F	431
DAVIS	Mary	16 OCT 1832	23 OCT 1832	H	180
DAVIS	Nancy	12 FEB 1833	26 FEB 1833	H	188
DAVIS	Nehemiah	3 JUN 1850	6 JUN 1850	K	473
DAVIS	Robert	20 MAY 1818	27 JUN 1818	G	118
DAVISON	William	4 DEC 1814	7 JUL 1820	G	169
DAWSON	William	19 AUG 1815	10 SEP 1815	G	60
DAWSON	Zebediah	10 MAR 1819	21 SEP 1819	G	154
DAZEY	John	23 SEP 1795	19 MAR 1811	F	449
DAZEY	Joseph	22 JUN 1843	11 JUL 1846	K	175
DAZEY	Moses	5 MAY 1848	7 MAY 1849	K	385

DEAN	Charles	7 AUG 1819	1 OCT 1819	G	160
DEPUTY	Jeremiah	22 JUN 1833	27 JUL 1845	K	106
DEPUTY	Sally	17 MAR 1819	1 MAY 1819	G	142
DEPUTY	Solomon	5 FEB 1824	17 NOV 1829	H	55
DEPUTY	Sylvester	2 APR 1804	21 DEC 1807	F	331
DERICKSON	John	1840	20 NOV 1840	I	237
DERICKSON	Leasha	? ? ? ?	11 OCT 1848	K	322
DERICKSON	William	1 JAN 1848	DEC 1850	K	499
DICKERSON	Alanson	8 DEC 1851	31 DEC 1851	K	570
DICKERSON	Charles	31 OCT 1836	12 JUN 1839	I	187
DICKERSON	Dorry	1 MAY 1816	21 MAY 1816	G	78
DICKERSON	Edmond	23 DEC 1831	4 JAN 1832	H	145
DICKERSON	Elisha	28 MAR 1848	9 NOV 1848	K	323
DICKERSON	Elizabeth	20 DEC 1836	17 MAR 1837	I	41
DICKERSON	Jonathan	29 AUG 1823	18 NOV 1823	G	302
DICKERSON	Jonathan	20 JAN 1835	8 MAY 1838	I	125
DINGLE	Betsey	18 FEB 1838	3 MAR 1838	I	102
DINGLE	Edward	10 DEC 1823	20 NOV 1824	G	358
DIRECKSON	Joseph	17 OCT 1832	24 OCT 1832	H	181
DISHROONE	Abigail	9 DEC 1805	14 JUN 1808	F	333
DIXSON	William	8 MAR 1813	31 MAY 1813	F	512
DODD	Aaron	3 APR 1799	22 MAY 1806	F	233
DODD	Absolem	26 AUG 1847	25 APR 1848	K	285
DODD	Mariam	27 JUN 1838	17 FEB 1842	I	320
DODD	Sarah	16 MAR 1812	26 MAR 1816	G	69
DOLBEY	Isaac	17 FEB 1844	23 APR 1844	K	33
DONOVAN	Abraham	28 AUG 1816	8 JUN 1818	G	112
DONOVAN	Foster	8 OCT 1821	27 MAY 1822	G	256
DONOVAN	Phillip	23 FEB 1842	28 NOV 1843	K	20
DONOVAN	Somerset	5 SEP 1849	21 SEP 1849	K	419
DRAIN	Soloman	12 MAY 1851	4 AUG 1851	K	555
DRAPER	John	21 JAN 1815	17 NOV 1817	G	99
DRAPER	John	? ? ? ?	4 SEP 1848	K	345
DRAPER	Maud	30 AUG 1823	9 DEC 1823	G	310
DRAPER	William	1 APR 1834	29 MAR 1842	I	332
DRYDEN	John	28 FEB 1810	20 MAR 1810	F	411
DUFY	Michael	31 JAN 1847	23 FEB 1847	K	222
DUTTON	Abel	29 AUG 1801	8 DEC 1801	E	307
DUTTON	Abel	11 MAR 1849	17 MAR 1849	K	356
DUTTON	John	7 FEB 1832	29 FEB 1832	H	160
DUTTON	Thomas	26 JAN 1830	8 FEB 1830	H	68
EDWARDS	Samuel	8 JUN 1801	17 MAY 1804	F	141
ELLEGOOD	Peggy	23 APR 1849	11 FEB 1851	K	505
ELLEGOOD	Thomas	9 JAN 1819	13 AUG 1822	G	264
ELLENSWORTH	Elijah	11 FEB 1848	7 MAR 1848	K	270
ELLIGOOD	Mary	13 JUL 1829	10 APR 1833	H	198
ELLIOTT	Daniel	27 AUG 1807	6 APR 1810	F	412
ELLIOTT	John	3 NOV 1807	15 DEC 1807	F	307
ELLIOTT	John	9 NOV 1804	25 JAN 1815	G	43

7

ELLIOTT	John	2 SEP 1832	2 OCT 1832	H	177
ELLIOTT	Joshua	26 APR 1837	18 DEC 1838	I	158
ELLIOTT	Samuel	16 FEB 1829	10 NOV 1829	H	53
ELLIOTT	Temperance	11 JUN 1844	22 SEP 1846	K	183
ELLIOTT	Thomas	9 APR 1832	20 APR 1839	I	178
ELLIS	Elizabeth	9 JUN 1814	5 JUL 1814	G	27
ELLIS	Stephen	27 JAN 1834	18 FEB 1834	H	231
ELLISS	George	7 APR 1837	5 FEB 1839	I	169
ELLISS	Stephen	2 APR 1801	5 SEP 1802	F	70
ELLISS	William	20 SEP 1837	21 NOV 1837	I	80
ENGLISH	Elisha	8 NOV 1850	17 MAR 1851	K	518
ENGLISH	James	8 SEP 1792	2 APR 1802	E	309
ENNIS	Rhoda	15 MAR 1825	31 MAY 1825	G	291
ENNISS	John	5 JUN 1813	12 JUL 1813	F	508
ENNISS	Purnal	20 JAN 1840	27 APR 1846	K	172
EVANS	Catherine	15 OCT 1812	22 DEC 1812	F	499
EVANS	Daniel	1 SEP 1790	10 NOV 1800	F	17
EVANS	Elisha	9 JAN 1834	29 SEP 1836	I	1
EVANS	Enoch	27 MAR 1847	17 AUG 1847	K	251
EVANS	John	11 NOV 1799	25 JAN 1800	E	256
EVANS	John	15 SEP 1809	10 OCT 1809	F	440
EVANS	John	12 JUN 1819	21 JUN 1819	G	146
FVANS	John	1 FEB 1842	26 JUL 1842	I	342
EVANS	John	11 JUL 1848	9 APR 1849	K	381
EVANS	Keziah	30 SEP 1812	12 OCT 1814	G	22
EVANS	Robert	24 JUL 1833	27 AUG 1833	H	210
EVANS	Soloman	6 JAN 1805	4 OCT 1808	F	344
EVANS	William	20 OCT 1810	22 JAN 1811	F	438
EVANS	William	8 OCT 1833	14 JAN 1834	H	224
EVANS	Jehu	16 MAR 1816	25 MAR 1816	G	71
EWING	Gustavus	18 DEC 1845	30 DEC 1845	K	137
EWINGS	Brinkley	12 JAN 1829	10 FEB 1829	H	34
FASSITT	William	14 DEC 1808	21 FEB 1809	F	360
FERGUS	Mary	22 JUL 1806	14 JAN 1812	F	484
FERMAN	James	26 FEB 1839	28 MAY 1839	i	182
FESSITT	Elijah	11 JUL 1798	23 SEP 1800	E	277
FICHELL	William	11 DEC 1800	7 JAN 1801	E	298
FISHER	Curtis	8 JUN 1825	24 JUN 1825	G	396
FISHER	Rachel	6 FEB 1800	31 MAR 1801	E	275
FISHER	Samuel	27 MAR 1820	8 OCT 1821	G	219
FITCHELL	Severn	18 JAN 1823	25 OCT 1825	G	403
FLEETWOOD	Abigail	27 SEP 1795	26 SEP 1815	G	61
FLEETWOOD	Elizabeth	9 DEC 1837	20 FEB 1838	I	98
FLEETWOOD	Whittington	4 FEB 1822	30 JUL 1822	G	260
FLEETWOOD	William	26 SEP 1821	25 OCT 1821	G	220
FOLK	Mary	1 APR 1797	5 SEP 1803	F	108
FOUNTAIN	Zebdiel	23 APR 1816	29 MAY 1816	G	72
FOWLER	Arthur	17 DEC 1814	2 JAN 1821	G	195
FOWLER	Jesse	2 MAY 1803	27 AUG 1804	F	161

8

FOWLER	Laurence	JAN 1843	24 JAN 1843	I	371
FRAME	John	7 MAY 1811	14 MAY 1811	F	461
FRAME	Robert	20 JUL 1801	15 JUL 1802	F	51
FRAMPTON	Hubert	18 APR 1815	9 MAY 1815	G	48
FREEMAN	Michael	5 NOV 1805	4 FEB 1806	F	217
FREEMAN	Moses	8 DEC 1838	27 DEC 1838	I	163
FREEMAN	Purnell	11 OCT 1831	10 APR 1832	H	165
FREEMAN	William	31 AUG 1830	8 MAY 1838	I	122
GAME	Morris	1 JUL 1850	7 AUG 1850	K	483
GIBBONS	Jonathan	23 NOV 1804	15 DEC 1804	F	172
GIBBONS	Josiah	29 JUL 1821	1 AUG 1821	G	215
GIBBS	Bunnaughs	3 JUN 1816	20 JUN 1816	G	29
GODWIN	Daniel	10 JAN 1832	28 AUG 1833	H	209
GORDON	George	29 APR 1809	30 JUN 1809	F	373
GORDON	Nathaniel	13 MAR 1810	12 OCT 1811	F	469
GORDY	Aaron	6 JUN 1812	23 DEC 1814	G	23
GORDY	Elizabeth	13 NOV 1834	15 MAR 1837	I	39
GORDY	Jackson	12 OCT 1834	22 JAN 1836	H	314
GORDY	John	20 FEB 1801	11 DEC 1801	F	36
GORDY	Thomas	12 DEC 1845	23 DEC 1845	K	134
GOSLEE	George	19 JAN 1829	10 AUG 1835	H	295
GOSLEE	George	10 AUG 1835	12 JAN 1837	I	18
GOSLEE	Job	11 DEC 1810	31 DEC 1810	F	434
GOSLEE	Nancy	18 APR 1832	8 MAY 1832	H	172
GOSLEE	William	28 1830	14 DEC 1833	H	219
GOSLEN	John	14 DEC 1843	5 FEB 1845	K	70
GRACE	John	12 MAY 1799	1 JUN 1802	F	1
GRAHAM	Nancy	30 JAN 1808	11 FEB 1811	F	444
GRAY	Peter	5 APR 1802	20 APR 1803	F	21
GRAY	William	2 DEC 1799	28 APR 1801	F	115
GREEN	Jesse	14 MAR 1834	9 SEP 1834	H	254
GREEN	Louise	26 NOV 1845	26 JAN 1847	K	215
GREENE	Richard	13 OCT 1800	8 MAY 1809	F	377
GRICE	Thomas	23 APR 1833	28 FEB 1843	I	375
GRIFFITH	Isaac	24 MAY 1831	13 APR 1841	I	261
GRIFFITH	James	25 JAN 1833	12 FEB 1833	H	187
GRIFFITH	John	6 JAN 1822	21 FEB 1822	G	240
GRIFFITH	Joseph	20 JUN 1810	17 JUN 1816	G	80
GRIFFITH	Joshua	7 DEC 1825	23 MAY 1826	G	421
GRIFFITH	Nancy	18 JUN 1832	19 MAR 1833	H	194
GRIFFITH	Samuel	21 JUL 1831	4 NOV 1833	H	220
GROVES	Jeremiah	11 JUL 1833	10 DEC 1833	H	218
GUNBY	Stephen	6 APR 1822	23 APR 1822	G	244
GURLEY	Francis	27 MAR 1830	6 APR 1830	H	78
HALL	Abigail	JUL 1794	21 APR 1804	F	150
HALL	Ann	6 APR 1835	1 JUN 1841	I	271
HALL	George	10 DEC 1834	7 NOV 1837	I	75
HALL	Given	16 NOV 1802	27 FEB 1809	F	364
HALL	Joseph	27 AUG 1805	20 SEP 1805	F	203

HALL	Joshua	16 MAR 1829	12 FEB 1833	H	186
HALL	Moses	20 DEC 1809	22 MAY 1810	F	404
HALL	Robert	18 FEB 1843	23 SEP 1843	K	1
HALL	William	27 MAY 1805	15 MAY 1817	G	97
HALLS	Sarah	? ? ? ?	1 SEP 1825	G	399
HAMMOND	Isaac	19 OCT 1811	18 NOV 1811	F	475
HANDCOCK	Micajah	27 AUG 1808	15 NOV 1808	F	356
HANDERSON	Abram	3 APR 1816	9 FEB 1821	G	197
HANDSOR	Nehemiah	13 SEP 1842	20 MAY 1845	K	102
HANDY	John	7 APR 1808	19 APR 1808	F	334
HANDY	Prudence	6 JUN 1827	13 JAN 1829	H	30
HANDZAR	John	7 OCT 1806	6 JAN 1807	F	249
HANSON	Thomas	18 MAY 1821	25 SEP 1821	G	216
HANSOR	William	25 MAR 1847	14 APR 1848	K	277
HANZAR	William	26 OCT 1785	22 DEC 1801	E	312
HARB	John	26 OCT 1801	30 OCT 1801	F	34
HARDEN	Nancy	? ? ? ?	1849	K	350
HARGIS	Abraham	13 APR 1811	20 SEP 1813	F	525
HARMAN	Elie	17 NOV 1818	19 NOV 1818	G	128
HARPER	Sarah	8 MAR 1849	19 MAY 1849	K	394
HARRIS	Benton	21 FEB 1820	24 JUN 1830	H	81
HARRIS	Isabel	3 APR 1839	7 MAY 1839	F	1
HARRIS	Isabel	3 APR 1839	7 MAY 1839	I	180
HARRIS	Peggy	11 SEP 1832	15 NOV 1836	I	10
HARRISON	George	10 FEB 1821	29 MAY 1826	G	422
HASELY	Sarah	6 AUG 1825	21 AUG 1826	G	428
HASSARD	Cord	9 FEB 1826	31 MAR 1831	H	105
HASTING	Daniel	11 JUL 1822	16 JUL 1822	G	259
HASTING	Frederick	13 NOV 1820	9 DEC 1824	G	365
HASTING	Jacob	21 JUN 1832	3 JUN 1833	H	204
HASTING	James	1830	12 MAR 1833	H	191
HASTING	Molly	27 AUG 1849	18 SEP 1849	K	417
HASTING	Polly	31 JAN 1845	22 OCT 1845	K	123
HASTING	Sovren	10 FEB 1827	8 MAY 1827	G	452
HASTING	William	15 APR 1817	5 FEB 1818	G	125
HASTINGS	Elijah	22 DEC 1840	15 AUG 1843	I	397
HASTINGS	Levi	5 AUG 1831	6 SEP 1831	H	124
HASTY	Nehemiah	9 DEC 1806	26 DEC 1806	F	263
HATFIELD	Zacheriah	9 JAN 1841	20 APR 1842	I	322
HAYES	Ann	14 JUL 1808	19 DEC 1809	F	388
HAYMAN	Isaac	17 FEB 1816	15 MAR 1816	G	69
HAYS	Alexander	9 JUN 1809	12 AUG 1809	F	376
HAZZARD	Ann	26 APR 1801	11 MAY 1801	E	286
HAZZARD	Arthur	30 APR 1800	13 MAY 1800	E	263
HAZZARD	Elihu	24 MAR 1805	20 AUG 1805	F	199
HAZZARD	George	13 OCT 1800	16 DEC 1800	E	272
HAZZARD	Jacob	8 APR 1808	28 JUN 1808	F	335
HAZZARD	Jane	17 JUL 1822	11 FEB 1823	G	276
HAZZARD	John	26 APR 1823	1 JAN 1826	G	412

10

HAZZARD	Lemuel	8 AUG 1812	21 JAN 1813	G	9
HAZZARD	Lydia	19 OCT 1847	14 MAR 1848	K	274
HAZZARD	Mary	28 DEC 1815	3 NOV 1819	G	156
HAZZARD	Mary	21 FEB 1839	30 DEC 1843	K	22
HAZZARD	Polly	14 DEC 1832	14 NOV 1838	I	155
HAZZARD	Selick	29 MAY 1826	9 MAR 1827	G	447
HEARN	George	31 MAR 1851	10 JUN 1851	K	525
HEARN	Harriet	17 OCT 1835	19 JAN 1836	H	312
HEARN	Jonathan	30 NOV 1820	10 JAN 1825	G	371
HEARN	Lavinia	20 JUL 1850	14 NOV 1850	K	494
HEARN	Samual	24 DEC 1802	8 JUL 1803	F	72
HEARN	Samuel	1846	15 APR 1850	K	465
HEARN	Theodore	15 AUG 1843	30 OCT 1843	K	13
HEARN	Thomas	4 MAY 1838	9 JUL 1838	I	131
HEARNE	Elizabeth	4 JAN 1804	3 AUG 1804	F	153
HEAVELO	Reuben	28 APR 1836	24 FEB 1837	I	34
HEAVELOE	Anthony	28 AUG 1818	1 JUN 1819	G	150
HEAVELOW	Anothony	8 SEP 1824	2 MAR 1825	G	379
HEAVERLO	Anthony	16 JUL 1804	22 OCT 1807	F	328
HEAVERLO	Margaret	22 SEP 1825	9 APR 1835	H	284
HEAVERLOW	Jessee	17 FEB 1830	16 MAR 1830	H	75
HEMMONS	John	APR 1821	7 JUN 1821	G	212
HEMMONS	Selah	21 NOV 1818	13 APR 1819	G	141
HENRY	George	6 JUL 1803	19 AUG 1803	F	103
HENRY	James	13 JAN 1846	3 FEB 1846	K	143
HERENS	Mary	15 MAY 1825	21 JUN 1825	G	394
HEVELO	Jonathan	21 JAN 1821	4 MAR 1823	G	280
HICKMAN	Ann	14 SEP 1796	29 JUN 1802	F	65
HICKMAN	Nicholas	31 MAR 1817	10 JUN 1817	G	100
HICKMAN	Selby	6 JUN 1851	7 OCT 1851	K	566
HICKMAN	Ward	29 MAY 1830	12 JUL 1830	H	85
HICKMAN	William	9 OCT 1828	23 JUL 1830	H	87
HIGMAN	Priscilla	2 MAR 1829	9 APR 1833	H	197
HILL	Arcada	20 JUN 1829	21 JUN 1829	H	125
HILL	Betsy	7 JAN 1800	19 NOV 1800	E	274
HILL	Brittingham	22 JAN 1801	9 AUG 1811	F	464
HINSON	John	10 SEP 1806	1 OCT 1806	F	240
HITCH	Robert	31 OCT 1844	19 NOV 1844	K	59
HITCHENS	Edmond	8 MAR 1823	14 OCT 1823	G	297
HITCHENS	Edmond	20 SEP 1831	5 OCT 1835	H	303
HITCHENS	Eunice	4 MAY 1849	7 NOV 1849	K	427
HITCHENS	Jarret	6 JUN 1818	6 OCT 1820	G	173
HITCHENS	Margaret	14 DEC 1821	DEC 1821	G	231
HOBBS	William	5 AUG 1837	13 OCT 1842	I	353
HOLLAND	Elizabeth	8 OCT 1839	12 NOV 1839	I	209
HOLLAND	Elzey	FEB 1849	5 MAR 1849	K	349
HOLLAND	Jacob	19 FEB 1803	9 MAR 1803	F	193
HOLLAND	John	25 OCT 1821	15 MAY 1822	G	251
HOLLAND	John	13 JUL 1837	29 AUG 1837	I	59

11

HOLLAND	Mary	1 MAR 1839	27 SEP 1841	I	285
HOLLAND	West	MAR 1809	11 DEC 1821	G	229
HOLLIS	Hinson	14 OCT 1806	19 NOV 1806	F	245
HOLLIS	Levina	18 SEP 1845	18 FEB 1846	K	149
HOLLIS	Sylva	26 JUN 1817	29 JUN 1817	G	95
HOOD	Mary	7 SEP 1816	29 OCT 1816	G	180
HOOD	Robert	25 JUL 1808	4 JUN 1811	F	459
HOOPER	Elizabeth	13 JAN 1849	24 JAN 1850	K	454
HOPKINS	John	23 FEB 1832	16 SEP 1833	H	211
HOPKINS	Levi	28 FEB 1837	13 NOV 1837	I	77
HOPKINS	Molly	14 OCT 1805	15 NOV 1805	F	209
HOPKINS	Philip	12 MAR 1805	21 SEP 1805	F	204
HOPKINS	Robert	9 DEC 1799	9 JUN 1802	F	78
HOPKINS	Robert	27 AUG 1807	20 OCT 1807	F	303
HOPKINS	Thomas	3 JUL 1799	16 FEB 1808	F	313
HORSEY	John	13 SEP 1827	16 OCT 1827	H	2
HORSEY	Revel	10 OCT 1824	16 NOV 1835	H	308
HORSEY	Stephen	10 JUN 1802	21 AUG 1802	E	287
HORSEY	Thomas	15 SEP 1849	25 SEP 1849	K	421
HOULSTON	Joseph	9 SEP 1798	4 FEB 1801	E	289
HOUSTON	John	4 JAN 1828	28 JAN 1828	H	10
HOUSTON	Joseph	3 APR 1821	24 APR 1821	G	206
HOUSTON	Joseph	28 DEC 1837	26 MAR 1845	K	90
HOUSTON	Priscillah	8 JAN 1814	8 MAR 1814	G	13
HOUSTON	Robert	19 AUG 1803	5 SEP 1803	F	102
HOUSTON	Robert	4 MAR 1821	16 JAN 1822	G	236
HOUSTON	William	17 APR 1819	15 JAN 1820	G	163
HOWARD	Comfort	8 MAR 1823	23 SEP 1823	G	295
HUDSON	Alexander	16 APR 1831	8 JUN 1831	H	118
HUDSON	Benjamin	1 DEC 1805	1 APR 1806	F	225
HUDSON	Benjamin	29 JAN 1840	31 MAR 1840	I	219
HUDSON	Daniel	24 APR 1851	4 OCT 1851	K	557
HUDSON	Elijah	11 DEC 1840	19 FEB 1841	I	253
HUDSON	Henry	14 AUG 1809	26 OCT 1813	G	1
HUDSON	Jaquish	3 OCT 1811	19 NOV 1811	F	473
HUDSON	John	18 JAN 1811	5 MAR 1811	F	453
HUDSON	Joseph	30 JUL 1813	24 NOV 1813	G	8
HUDSON	Joseph	28 AUG 1825	30 SEP 1826	G	439
HUDSON	Lucretia	4 MAY 1814	23 MAY 1814	G	13
HUDSON	Mary	3 APR 1803	20 FEB 1807	F	252
HUDSON	Nehemme	16 JUL 18--	31 AUG 1824	G	347
HUDSON	Sally	27 JUN 1849	13 OCT 1851	K	579
HUDSON	Samuel	21 FEB 1840	14 OCT 1840	I	233
HUDSON	Sarah	3 DEC 1816	7 JAN 1817	G	104
HUFFINGTON	William	27 MAY 1819	18 JUN 1819	G	148
HUGHES	David	13 FEB 1820	4 MAY 1820	G	167
HUGHES	John	27 AUG 1820	19 SEP 1820	G	173
HUGHES	Philip	24 NOV 1803	16 DEC 1803	F	117
HUGHES	Whitefield	4 JAN 1829	21 APR 1829	H	41

HURLEY	Caty	7 MAY 1812	28 SEP 1821	G	218
HURLEY	Charles	30 AUG 1817	4 NOV 1817	G	102
HURLEY	Edmond	4 FEB 1796	15 FEB 1812	F	487
HURST	Samuel	17 AUG 1847	28 AUG 1847	K	353
INGRAM	Joshua	11 JAN 1822	15 JAN 1822	G	235
INSLEY	Asbury	6 JUL 1839	25 JUL 1839	I	189
INSLEY	John	25 SEP 1816	25 OCT 1816	G	103
IRELAND	Samuel	5 JAN 1809	24 JAN 1809	F	355
IRONS	Lemuel	27 JUL 1836	24 JUL 1840	I	226
JACKSON	Elizabeth	24 OCT 1805	27 NOV 1805	F	212
JACKSON	Julius	29 JAN 1800	8 OCT 1801	F	14
JACKSON	Mary	23 FEB 1835	15 FEB 1837	I	32
JACOB	Nancy	21 APR 1836	14 MAR 1837	I	36
JACOBS	Curtis	7 NOV 1829	26 MAY 1831	H	109
JACOBS	John	FEB 1824	22 FEB 1825	G	378
JACOBS	Sauballet	14 DEC 1847	11 JUL 1848	K	302
JACOBS	William	26 SEP 1811	30 SEP 1811	F	468
JAMES	Jehu	26 JUL 1832	11 OCT 1832	H	178
JAMES	John	10 JAN 1827	29 DEC 1827	H	7
JAMES	Joshua	10 OCT 1800	11 JUN 1805	F	196
JEFFERSON	Job	20 MAR 1819	26 AUG 1828	H	22
JEFFERSON	John	1822	1 FEB 1825	G	377
JEFFERSON	Nancy	30 SEP 1836	17 JAN 1838	I	86
JEFFERSON	Warren	25 SEP 1845	1848	K	297
JEFFERSON	William	16 AUG 1835	20 AUG 1835	H	296
JEFFERSON	William	1 SEP 1836	19 JUN 1838	I	127
JERMAN	Joshua	1 OCT 1837	1 FEB 1838	I	91
JESTER	Daniel	26 JUN 1831	21 JAN 1840	I	214
JESTER	Daniel	25 MAY 1850	11 JUN 1850	K	477
JESTER	Elias	6 NOV 1814	15 NOV 1814	G	20
JOHNSON	Benjamin	30 SEP 1801	9 FEB 1802	E	284
JOHNSON	Benjamin	9 MAR 1811	31 JUL 1821	G	213
JOHNSON	Isaiah	10 JAN 1809	29 JUN 1809	F	374
JOHNSON	Job	26 JAN 1800	11 MAR 1800	E	256
JOHNSON	John	10 JAN 1838	9 MAR 1838	I	107
JOHNSON	John	8 APR 1848	13 JUN 1848	K	294
JOHNSON	Joseph	15 FEB 1803	15 MAR 1803	F	92
JOHNSON	Joshua	4 OCT 1840	24 OCT 1840	I	240
JOHNSON	Purnal	13 AUG 1844	24 AUG 1844	K	39
JOHNSON	Rachel	21 AUG 1813	18 MAY 1819	G	145
JOHNSON	Samuel	28 FEB 1800	22 MAR 1800	E	262
JOHNSON	Samuel	19 SEP 1834	12 DEC 1834	H	268
JOHNSON	Tilghnan	No Date	5 JAN 1835	H	270
JOHNSON	William	1 DEC 1797	11 NOV 1802	F	86
JOHNSON	William	10 JUN 1837	9 MAR 1838	I	105
JOHNSON	William	21 FEB 1834	4 OCT 1844	K	50
JONES	Ann	7 JUN 1798	16 DEC 1801	E	288
JONES	Hannah	14 AUG 1817	11 NOV 1845	K	129
JONES	Jacob	14 FEB 1826	30 JAN 1828	H	12

13

JONES	Mary	23 FEB 1800	14 OCT 1800	E	295
JONES	Nehemiah	3 SEP 1803	3 AUG 1813	F	523
JONES	William	6 MAY 1845	11 MAY 1850	K	488
JOSEPH	Hezekiah	25 JUN 1832	5 JUL 1832	H	173
JOSEPH	Jeremiah	14 FEB 1824	27 NOV 1824	G	361
JOSEPH	Jonathan	28 MAR 1831	11 MAY 1835	H	292
JOSEPH	Nathan	19 JUL 1822	22 FEB 1831	H	100
JUMP	Olive	30 DEC 1810	5 FEB 1811	F	442
KELLAM	Jesse	12 NOV 1805	26 NOV 1805	F	211
KENDRICK	William	28 DEC 1842	6 JAN 1843	I	365
KERSHAW	John	30 SEP 1837	31 OCT 1837	I	89
KERSHAW	Mitchell	24 NOV 1815	19 JAN 1819	G	127
KINDER	Jacob	10 MAY 1837	19 SEP 1837	I	62
KING	Elizabeth	1 JUN 1837	1 AUG 1838	I	139
KING	John	19 MAY 1833	10 JUN 1837	I	55
KING	Samuel	24 FEB 1814	24 FEB 1816	G	66
KINGDON	Joseph	10 SEP 1809	19 OCT 1809	F	422
KINNAKIN	Sarah	8 JAN 1813	26 JAN 1813	G	12
KINNEY	Elijah	7 APR 1806	20 JUN 1806	F	261
KINNIKIN	Waitman	13 SEP 1824	28 SEP 1824	G	251
KNOLES	Richard	28 NOV 1836	7 FEB 1837	I	25
KNOWLES	Isaac	7 APR 1846	4 AUG 1846	K	181
KNOWLES	Marvel	4 MAR 1838	20 SEP 1843	I	403
KNOWLES	Robert	10 OCT 1820	30 OCT 1821	G	225
KOLLOCK	Jane	5 AUG 18--	1804	F	192
KOLLOCK	Phillips	23 JUN 1824	2 JUL 1824	G	341
KOLLOCK	Simon	12 JUN 1816	14 JUN 1817	G	105
LACEY	Robert	9 AUG 1816	13 NOV 1826	G	443
LACEY	Spencer	10 MAR 1810	10 JUL 1823	G	293
LAFERDY	Samual	No Date	24 APR 1804	F	152
LAMBDON	Robert	25 SEP 1807	29 SEP 1813	F	524
LANE	John	13 JUL 1815	9 OCT 1815	G	59
LANGRILL	John	17 DEC 1807	14 DEC 1808	F	359
LANK	Alcie	21 AUG 1821	28 AUG 1821	G	216
LANK	Lovisa	7 FEB 1843	16 DEC 1844	K	61
LANK	Thomas	3 APR 1837	14 FEB 1838	I	109
LAWS	Daniel	19 JAN 1808	18 FEB 1808	F	316
LAWS	Jacob	18 OCT 1831	25 OCT 1831	H	134
LAWS	Joshua	27 MAR 1821	24 APR 1821	G	205
LAWSON	James	11 DEC 1828	21 MAY 1829	H	43
LAYTON	Eli	26 JUL 1840	2 SEP 1845	K	111
LAYTON	Hughitt	1 JAN 1802	24 APR 1802	F	58
LAYTON	Joshua	21 JUN 1848	2 APR 1849	K	363
LAYTON	Lowder	23 JUN 1849	3 JUL 1849	K	400
LAYTON	Nancy	19 SEP 1843	17 APR 1845	K	98
LAYTON	Purnal	6 APR 1846	17 APR 1846	K	164
LAYTON	Sally	18 AUG 1825	7 JUL 1828	H	20
LAYTON	Tilghman	25 SEP 1811	25 NOV 1811	F	476
LAYTON	William	18 NOV 1816	7 JAN 1817	G	89

14

LEARNMONTH	John	7 AUG 1802	17 SEP 1802	F	69
LECAT	Ebenezer	28 JAN 1848	13 MAR 1851	K	513
LECAT	Shadrack	? ? ? ?	1849	K	341
LECATT	Gustavus	22 FEB 1815	9 MAY 1817	G	181
LEVERTON	Richard	8 JAN 1808	2 FEB 1808	F	308
LEWIS	Job	16 APR 1807	10 DEC 1807	F	306
LIGHT	Thomas	2 FEB 1804	14 MAY 1804	F	148
LINCH	Abram	31 DEC 1830	22 FEB 1831	H	101
LINCH	Eli	8 SEP 1832	28 SEP 1836	I	7
LINCH	Jacob	13 APR 1808	30 AUG 1808	F	342
LINCH	John	12 NOV 1846	12 NOV 1846	K	204
LINCH	Joseph	28 SEP 1843	4 NOV 1843	K	16
LINDALL	Zadock	5 DEC 1804	22 JAN 1805	F	175
LINGO	Henry	26 FEB 1831	1 MAR 1831	H	102
LINGO	John	7 JUN 1827	8 AUG 1827	H	1
LINGO	Samuel	7 JUN 1834	29 JUL 1834	H	250
LINGO	Smith	13 MAR 1806	28 MAR 1806	F	262
LINGREL	Nehemiah	4 JUL 1825	11 JUL 1825	G	397
LITTLETON	Charles	1 NOV 1811	6 JAN 1812	F	482
LITTLETON	Edmund	11 MAY 1829	26 MAY 1829	H	46
LOCKWOOD	Benjamin	20 APR 1809	8 AUG 1822	G	261
LOCKWOOD	Mary	8 JUN 1820	6 APR 1824	G	323
LOCKWOOD	Samuel	21 JAN 1802	12 OCT 1807	F	324
LOFLAND	Elias	9 NOV 1829	22 DEC 1829	H	56
LOFLAND	Gabriel	19 JUN 1817	25 JUN 1817	G	98
LOFLAND	Grace	5 JUN 1799	14 OCT 1801	E	306
LOFLAND	James	17 OCT 1816	19 NOV 1816	G	81
LOFLAND	John	12 JAN 1800	27 AUG 1801	E	303
LOFLAND	Joshua	6 OCT 1834	3 FEB 1835	H	272
LOFLAND	Margaret	28 JUN 1808	20 JUL 1808	F	338
LOFLAND	William	7 APR 1815	7 NOV 1816	G	58
LONG	Benjamin	17 NOV 1797	4 FEB 1800	E	254
LONG	Eber	31 JUL 1848	29 AUG 1848	K	312
LONG	George	4 NOV 1819	25 FEB 1820	G	164
LONG	James	1 MAR 1839	5 MAR 1839	I	166
LOW	Catherine	13 OCT 1843	6 NOV 1844	K	57
LOW	Zacheriah	24 SEP 1845	16 MAY 1848	K	292
LOWE	Thomas	25 MAR 1814	15 APR 1814	G	32
LOWE	Unice	24 AUG 1835	29 MAR 1837	I	43
LOYD	Wootten	5 FEB 1828	6 JUN 1833	H	205
LUDENUM	Aben	13 MAR 1807	23 APR 1807	F	280
LUDENUM	Rosannah	19 APR 1824	20 JUL 1824	G	339
LUDENUM	Thomas	27 MAR 1807	29 MAR 1808	F	327
MACKLIN	Job	7 NOV 1812	17 NOV 1812	F	504
MACKLIN	Jonathan	24 NOV 1834	14 MAR 1835	H	279
MAGEE	Besnard	7 DEC 1815	22 FEB 1816	G	64
MARAIN	Jacob	14 SEP 1829	7 MAR 1831	H	103
MARSH	Ann	3 NOV 1849	19 NOV 1849	K	450
MARSH	John	3 OCT 1849	13 NOV 1849	K	446

15

MARSH	Joseph	11 FEB 1831	3 APR 1832	H	162
MARSH	Peter	30 DEC 1812	4 AUG 1813	G	4
MARSH	Peter	8 MAY 1814	17 AUG 1814	G	17
MARSH	Peter	15 JAN 1850	1 SEP 1851	K	549
MARSH	Thomas	1 APR 1816	12 MAY 1821	G	208
MARSHALL	Aaron	1 SEP 1837	3 AUG 1839	I	191
MARSHALL	William	13 FEB 1844	14 NOV 1850	K	492
MARTIN	Elizabeth	3 FEB 1807	24 FEB 1807	F	257
MARTIN	James	1 MAY 1839	19 OCT 1846	K	193
MARTIN	John	29 NOV 1803	12 MAR 1805	F	183
MARVEL	Aaron	30 MAY 1833	17 MAY 1836	H	329
MARVEL	Adam	22 NOV 1829	26 MAY 1830	H	80
MARVEL	Comfort	20 SEP 1800	9 MAR 1802	F	32
MARVEL	Joseph	14 MAR 1817	15 APR 1817	G	92
MARVEL	Obediah	19 NOV 1834	11 DEC 1834	H	267
MARVEL	Philip	9 JAN 1850	27 AUG 1850	K	485
MARVEL	Thomas	28 JAN 1797	15 JAN 1801	E	311
MARVEL	Thomas	8 NOV 1829	15 SEP 1836	H	342
MARVEL	William	26 JUL 1847	15 FEB 1848	K	264
MARVEL	William	27 APR 1847	2 MAY 1848	K	288
MARVELL	Robert	17 JUL 1817	5 FEB 1824	G	317
MASSEY	John	23 APR 1804	17 OCT 1807	F	300
MASSEY	Lovey	24 JUL 1846	31 JUL 1849	K	408
MATTHEWS	Philip	18 NOV 1839	25 DEC 1846	K	207
MAULL	Joseph	3 MAY 1846	18 MAY 1846	K	168
MAXWELL	Elizabeth	3 MAY 1806	16 DEC 1806	F	247
MAY	Elizabeth	12 MAY 1808	28 FEB 1809	F	365
Mc CABE	Amos	1 AUG 1802	22 MAR 1825	G	382
McCABE	Arthur	18 AUG 18--	23 JAN 1843	I	367
McCAY	William	No Date	18 MAR 1800	E	257
McCOLLEY	Robert	12 MAR 1811	26 DEC 1811	F	477
McCRACKEN	John	9 JUL 1818	6 FEB 1819	G	182
McILVAIN	Benjamin	8 JAN 1846	14 JAN 1846	K	141
McILVAIN	Benjamin	4 OCT 1843	30 OCT 1847	K	259
McILVAIN	Comfort	3 AUG 1805	14 SEP 1807	F	294
McILVAIN	David	17 NOV 1828	11 FEB 1829	H	35
McILVAIN	James	11 SEP 1830	8 MAR 1834	H	237
McILVAIN	William	1826	OCT 1826	G	440
McILVAIN	Wrixsom	25 JAN 1844	22 AUG 1848	K	308
MEGEE	Rebecca	7 DEC 1815	19 DEC 1815	G	59
MELONEY	William	24 DEC 1831	23 JUL 1832	H	175
MELSON	John	10 DEC 1820	28 JAN 1822	G	237
MELSON	Joseph	22 FEB 1808	5 DEC 1809	F	382
MELSON	Joseph	18 JUL 1826	8 AUG 1826	G	426
MELSON	Thomas	9 NOV 1847	15 MAY 1849	K	388
MERINE	Matthew	21 OCT 1810	30 OCT 1810	F	423
MERINE	William	17 DEC 1831	23 DEC 1831	H	144
MESSICK	Coventon	9 JUN 1828	31 DEC 1828	H	29
MESSICK	Hannah	15 MAY 1832	3 MAR 1839	I	168

16

MESSICK	John	1 JAN 1825	10 APR 1827	G	449
MESSICK	Levi	5 FEB 1818	2 FEB 1819	G	136
MESSICK	Miles	No Date	9 AUG 1813	G	19
METCALF	John	14 JAN 1801	26 FEB 1801	E	291
MILBY	Ann	21 JAN 1803	31 May 1803	F	9
MILBY	George	No Date	26 MAY 1851	K	529
MILLER	James	18 OCT 1838	9 SEP 1841	I	280
MILLS	Jonathan	6 OCT 1818	17 NOV 1818	G	152
MINORS	Sarah	5 JUL 1848	5 OCT 1848	K	318
MITCHELL	Aba	1 MAR 1816	4 MAR 1816	G	67
MITCHELL	George	13 SEP 1798	27 APR 1799	F	320
MITCHELL	Hepsy	3 MAR 1824	21 MAR 1825	G	381
MITCHELL	John	6 MAY 1815	6 DEC 1816	G	83
MITCHELL	Rhoda	14 MAY 1818	19 MAY 1818	G	110
MITCHELL	Stephen	1 DEC 1810	31 DEC 1811	F	501
MITCHELL	Thomas	2 SEP 1844	6 JAN 1845	K	63
MITTEN	Ann	13 NOV 1805	3 DEC 1805	F	213
MITTEN	William	28 MAR 1803	3 MAY 1803	F	42
MOORE	Charles	22 APR 1817	31 OCT 1817	G	95
MOORE	Charles	7 APR 1832	24 MAR 1834	H	237
MOORE	Elzey	7 NOV 1832	21 MAR 1835	H	283
MOORE	George	14 JUL 1805	30 AUG 1805	F	200
MOORE	Isaac	15 FEB 1800	20 SEP 1803	F	112
MOORE	Luther	28 OCT 1830	11 DEC 1830	H	97
MOORE	Matthias	SEP 1818	30 NOV 1821	G	227
MOORE	William	1821	20 SEP 1824	G	350
MOORE	William	22 NOV 1822	11 APR 1826	G	418
MOORE	William	15 DEC 1836	11 JAN 1837	I	15
MORE	George	21 MAR 1846	20 APR 1846	K	170
MORGAN	David	21 MAR 1831	31 MAR 1831	H	104
MORGAN	Elijah	22 SEP 1813	3 DEC 1813	G	102
MORGAN	George	11 NOV 1831	12 DEC 1831	H	140
MORINE	David	1 AUG 1812	1 SEP 1812	F	492
MORRIS	Ann	12 AUG 1843	18 OCT 1844	K	51
MORRIS	Bevans	23 MAR 1819	21 FEB 1822	G	241
MORRIS	Burton	3 SEP 1835	6 OCT 1835	H	306
MORRIS	Cornelius	26 FEB 1834	17 APR 1845	K	93
MORRIS	Hezekiah	2 JAN 1824	3 FEB 1824	G	315
MORRIS	Jacob	13 JAN 1844	14 MAY 1847	K	232
MORRIS	Jeremiah	5 SEP 1833	20 JAN 1835	H	271
MORRIS	John	1 JAN 1822	15 DEC 1824	G	367
MORRIS	John	5 JUN 1833	20 JUN 1833	H	205
MORRIS	Jonathan	16 NOV 1837	17 APR 1840	I	224
MORRIS	Joshua	18 JAN 1800	19 MAR 1802	F	64
MORRIS	Joshua	17 MAR 1806	22 APR 1806	F	227
MORRIS	Joshua	30 OCT 1808	22 NOV 1808	F	350
MORRIS	Joshua	No Date	31 MAY 1842	I	334
MORRIS	Lacey	9 JUL 1814	14 NOV 1820	G	191
MORRIS	Mary	No Date	19 NOV 1823	G	303

MORRIS	Mary	14 MAY 1831	25 MAY 1831	H	117
MORRIS	Mary	20 APR 1832	25 MAY 1832	H	173
MORRIS	Mason	27 FEB 1830	13 MAR 1830	H	74
MORRIS	Robert	4 DEC 1817	9 JAN 1818	G	121
MORRIS	Susan	22 OCT 1842	30 SEP 1845	K	116
MORRIS	Willaim	30 APR 1815	17 FEB 1818	G	131
MORRIS	William	12 MAY 1821	23 JUN 1828	H	17
MORRIS	William	28 NOV 1832	5 MAR 1833	H	189
MORRISON	Hugh	28 MAR 1800	7 APR 1800	E	265
MORRISS	Curtis	2 MAR 1804	20 MAR 1804	F	126
MORRISS	John	3 APR 1804	3 MAY 1804	F	138
MUMFORD	John	24 APR 1821	30 OCT 1821	G	222
MUMFORD	William	20 JUL 1843	28 MAY 1844	K	37
MURPHY	Elizabeth	8 OCT 1831	14 NOV 1831	H	138
MURPHY	Hannah	2 NOV 1802	13 MAY 1814	G	176
MURPHY	Shadrack	16 JUN 1840	18 AUG 1840	I	228
MURRAY	David	1 SEP 1823	18 OCT 1823	G	299
MURRAY	James	6 MAR 1813	12 APR 1819	G	141
MURRAY	Nancv	27 APR 1847	29 JUN 1847	K	240
NEAL	John	5 APR 1802	9 AUG 1803	F	24
NEAL	John	20 AUG 1842	28 SEP 1842	I	344
NEAL	Joseph	16 FEB 1828	17 JUN 1839	I	184
NEAL	Polly	4 JAN 1835	4 AUG 1835	H	294
NEAL	William	24 APR 1806	27 AUG 1807	F	292
NEAL	William	31 MAR 1832	4 MAR 1834	H	233
NEWBOLD	James	24 AUG 1831	30 AUG 1831	H	123
NEWBOLD	William	12 FEB 1800	19 MAR 1800	E	259
NEWCOMB	Elizabeth	31 AUG 1786	10 NOV 1804	F	167
NEWTON	William	19 SEP 1806	18 MAR 1807	F	271
NICHOLSON	Huffington	11 JUN 1825	21 DEC 1825	G	406
NICHOLSON	Mary	6 MAY 1820	16 FEB 1830	H	70
NIELLE	Henry	1 NOV 1798	28 NOV 1803	F	119
NIELLE	Mary	29 NOV 1803	24 SEP 1803	F	122
NOBLE	Sarah	14 APR 1843	2 MAY 1843	I	384
NUNEZ	Hannah	19 AUG 1816	24 JUN 1819	G	151
O'NEAL	Thomas	1811	11 APR 1815	G	49
OBIER	Joshua	16 FEB 1809	28 FEB 1809	F	362
OKEY	William	24 OCT 1807	12 NOV 1807	F	297
OLIVER	Jean	17 MAR 1805	9 APR 1805	F	187
OTWELL	William	4 JUL 1833	15 APR 1834	H	240
OWENS	David	7 JUL 1810	20 AUG 1810	F	416
OWENS	Jean	15 JAN 1803	17 JAN 1805	F	178
OWENS	John	1820	1823	G	294
OWENS	John	7 JAN 1842	15 JUN 1847	K	237
OWENS	Robert	23 MAR 1802	21 NOV 1804	F	169
OWENS	Warrington	6 JAN 1811	24 MAR 1812	F	485
OZBUN	Leah	14 JUL 1808	16 AUG 1808	F	341
PARAMORE	Stephen	21 JUL 1819	7 NOV 1821	G	226
PARKER	George	7 MAR 1832	17 SEP 1833	H	212

PARKER	George	14 JUL 1841	27 OCT 1842	I	358
PARKER	John	25 NOV 1835	3 MAY 1836	H	327
PARKER	Richard	? ? ? ?	1849	K	343
PASSWATERS	Richard	MAR 1832	4 DEC 1838	I	157
PAYNTER	John	20 JUN 1843	19 AUG 1845	K	108
PAYNTER	Nathan	13 NOV 1837	15 FEB 1838	I	94
PAYNTER	Richard	15 DEC 1830	20 JUL 1831	H	122
PAYNTER	Samuel	14 SEP 1814	9 JAN 1815	G	44
PAYNTER	Samuel	24 JUN 1845	14 OCT 1845	K	115
PAYNTER	William	9 JAN 1845	10 APR 1845	K	91
PEARCE	Sarah	23 SEP 1829	10 NOV 1829	H	51
PEERY	James	10 JUN 1830	1 FEB 1831	H	99
PEERY	Margaret	18 JUN 1822	2 JAN 1823	G	274
PENNEWELL	David	17 JUN 1831	5 NOV 1831	H	135
PEPER	Joshua	12 AUG 1806	14 MAR 1809	F	497
PEPPER	John	7 JAN 1807	11 APR 1807	F	274
PERKINS	Mary	11 NOV 1801	22 MAY 1807	F	283
PETTIJOHN	Susanna	26 SEP 1848	7 OCT 1848	K	320
PETTIT	Rachel	5 FEB 1805	2 APR 1805	F	186
PETTYJOHN	George	28 SEP 1840	12 OCT 1840	I	232
PETTYJOHN	James	3 MAY 1794	3 DEC 1801	F	55
PETTYJOHN	Theodore	? ? ? ?	1849	K	352
PETTYJOHN	Thomas	5 FEB 1849	10 FEB 1849	K	333
PHILLIPS	Elijah	8 APR 1833	4 APR 1837	I	48
PHILLIPS	Isaac	19 FEB 1831	14 JUN 1831	H	118
PHILLIPS	James	27 JUN 1844	11 APR 1849	K	376
PHILLIPS	John	19 JUL 1819	7 SEP 1819	G	154
PHILLIPS	Joseph	2 JUN 1814	12 JAN 1815	G	41
PHILLIPS	Kendal	15 SEP 1840	21 NOV 1840	I	246
PHILLIPS	Molly	5 FEB 1844	27 FEB 1844	K	25
PHILLIPS	Nancy	25 FEB 1851	12 MAR 1851	K	521
PHILLIPS	Purnal	20 MAY 1812	10 JUN 1812	F	517
PHILLIPS	Richard	16 JUN 1818	28 JUL 1820	G	168
PHILLIPS	Richard	29 AUG 1823	21 OCT 1823	G	300
PHILLIPS	Samuel	24 APR 1824	11 JUN 1824	G	327
PHILLIPS	Shepherd	9 MAY 1800	14 MAY 1800	E	264
PHILLIPS	William	No Date	30 MAR 1843	I	377
PIERCE	John	3 OCT 1828	1838	I	151
PIERCE	John	17 FEB 1845	1 MAR 1845	K	85
PIERCE	Rebecca	20 MAY 1836	28 JUN 1836	H	331
POLK	Alexander	15 FEB 1807	11 MAR 1807	F	288
POLK	Charles	15 MAR 1813	7 MAR 1815	G	55
POLK	Elizabeth	14 FEB 1842	16 APR 1842	I	327
POLK	John	5 JAN 1842	18 OCT 1842	I	349
POLK	Kettura	21 DEC 1806	6 JAN 1807	F	248
POLK	Mary	23 JAN 1841	6 MAR 1841	I	259
POLK	William	8 FEB 1835	5 MAY 1835	H	288
POOL	Andrew	2 JAN 1802	15 JAN 1803	E	310
POOL	Perry	3 DEC 1831	20 JAN 1832	H	148

POSTELS	Thomas	13 OCT 1818	23 OCT 1827	H	3
POTTER	John	14 AUG 1830	2 SEP 1830	H	89
POUL	Edward	19 NOV 1800	27 NOV 1800	F	76
POWDERS	William	31 JUL 1803	23 AUG 1803	F	106
POWELL	Levi	24 NOV 1831	6 FEB 1832	H	155
POYNTER	Jane	3 SEP 1830	24 MAY 1831	H	116
PRETTYMAN	Benjamin	1823	16 SEP 1824	G	348
PRETTYMAN	Elizabeth	28 APR 1847	25 SEP 1850	K	490
PRETTYMAN	George	5 FEB 1797	18 APR 1804	F	139
PRETTYMAN	Jacob	24 MAR 1836	1 MAR 1845	K	87
PRETTYMAN	John	4 MAR 1823	11 MAR 1823	G	281
PRETTYMAN	John	No Date	20 DEC 1831	H	142
PRETTYMAN	Joseph	3 JAN 1804	10 JAN 1804	F	149
PRETTYMAN	Margaret	13 AUG 1830	20 JUN 1831	H	121
PRETTYMAN	Mary	2 APR 1832	11 APR 1832	H	166
PRETTYMAN	Peter	25 MAR 1847	31 MAY 1847	K	235
PRETTYMAN	Robert	12 MAY 1809	6 JUN 1810	F	406
PRETTYMAN	Robert	5 OCT 1836	26 JUL 1851	K	543
PRETTYMAN	Shephard	17 JAN 1833	20 JUL 1836	H	333
PRETTYMAN	Thomas	2 MAR 1802	16 JUN 1801	F	3
PRETTYMAN	Thomas	29 JUN 1814	19 JUL 1814	G	31
PRETTYMAN	William	12 MAY 1819	15 JAN 1822	G	232
PRETTYMAN	William	2 APR 1831	7 APR 1831	H	107
PRICE	George	20 DEC 1816	3 JAN 1817	G	90
PRIDE	Job	26 MAR 1819	30 MAR 1819	G	138
PRIITCHARD	James	25 MAR 1812	18 MAR 1814	G	37
PRITCHARD	John	8 JAN 1803	1 APR 1803	F	154
PRYTTAMAN	Elizabeth	8 DEC 1820	18 JUL 1825	G	397
PUSEY	John	20 JUL 1849	25 FEB 1851	K	511
PUSEY	Willaim	4 DEC 1805	No Date	G	134
QUILLEN	Joseph	17 DEC 1828	3 FEB 1829	H	32
RALPH	Charles	18 JUL 1845	28 OCT 1845	K	127
RALPH	Mary	10 FEB 1826	30 MAR 1830	H	75
RATLIFF	Elizabeth	27 JUN 1809	22 AUG 1809	F	398
RATLIFF	William	27 JAN 1800	28 JAN 1800	E	253
RECORDS	Thomas	26 OCT 1805	6 NOV 1805	F	208
RECORDS	Thomas	24 MAY 1815	24 NOV 1815	G	177
REDDEN	Polly	15 FEB 1850	18 FEB 1850	K	457
REDDING	Stephen	4 MAY 1800	21 JAN 1800	E	251
REED	Abraham	20 FEB 1838	17 APR 1838	I	118
REED	Benjamin	6 OCT 1803	28 DEC 1803	F	123
REED	James	11 DEC 1808	9 JAN 1809	F	353
REED	John	27 JUL 1824	2 JAN 1838	I	84
REED	Judah	5 MAY 1800	8 OCT 1800	E	267
REED	Manlove	21 NOV 1800	26 DEC 1800	E	273
REED	Mary	1 JUN 1812	23 APR 1817	G	94
REED	Rody	4 FEB 1810	7 FEB 1810	F	394
REYNOLDS	Thomas	14 SEP 1810	25 MAY 1812	F	494
REYNOLDS	Zachariah	21 MAY 1833	23 MAY 1834	H	245

RICARDS	Loxley	23 DEC 1802	15 MAR 1803	F	22
RICARDS	Thomas	26 JUL 1841	30 JUL 1841	I	275
RICCORDS	Joseph	24 JAN 1801	24 MAR 1801	E	276
RICHARDS	David	20 DEC 1801	6 MAR 1815	G	56
RICHARDS	Edward	28 MAR 1844	25 OCT 1845	K	120
RICHARDS	Elisha	10 OCT 1800	19 NOV 1800	E	296
RICHARDS	Elizabeth	7 MAR 1834	8 APR 1834	H	239
RICHARDS	Jacob	23 NOV 1826	30 APR 1833	H	200
RICHARDS	Joseph	9 APR 1804	24 APR 1804	F	136
RICHARDS	William	29 DEC 1790	14 OCT 1800	E	279
RICKARDS	Eli	25 DEC 1832	1 JAN 1834	H	221
RICKARDS	Elisha	10 OCT 1800	19 NOV 1800	E	320
RICKARDS	Elizabeth	22 AUG 1804	13 JAN 1809	F	351
RICKARDS	James	10 AUG 1831	6 SEP 1831	H	124
RICKARDS	Mary	3 SEP 1809	3 APR 1810	F	400
RICKARDS	Rachel	4 FEB 1846	20 APR 1846	K	166
RICKARDS	Thomas	28 MAR 1821	10 DEC 1822	G	273
RICORDS	Jammey	5 FEB 1832	30 MAR 1837	I	45
RIDER	Thomas	21 FEB 1826	13 MAR 1826	G	429
RIGGEN	Benjamin	15 MAY 1836	12 AUG 1836	H	337
RIGGS	Emelia	No Date	5 JUN 1823	G	290
RIGGS	Levi	9 FEB 1817	8 MAR 1817	G	101
RILEY	William	27 DEC 1801	30 DEC 1801	F	30
ROACH	Daniel	13 FEB 1812	18 MAR 1812	F	510
ROACH	William	18 OCT 1824	1 DEC 1824	G	363
ROADS	Margaret	25 JUN 1830	11 MAY 1847	K	230
ROBBINS	John	7 APR 1848	23 APR 1851	K	523
ROBBINS	Wiliam	17 APR 1819	22 JUN 1819	G	157
ROBERTS	Adam	MAY 1797	12 JAN 1802	F	63
ROBERTS	Harriet	30 JUN 1826	28 APR 1837	I	53
ROBERTS	Saunders	3 SEP 1801	12 MAR 1802	E	308
ROBINS	Abigal	21 JUN 1827	26 OCT 1832	H	182
ROBINSON	Ann	2 MAR 1817	24 JUN 1818	G	97
ROBINSON	Benjamin	14 AUG 1804	27 AUG 1804	F	157
ROBINSON	Joseph	2 JUN 1810	23 NOV 1815	G	62
ROBINSON	Joshua	18 OCT 1834	1 MAY 1838	I	120
ROBINSON	Mary	19 MAR 1835	22 APR 1835	H	285
ROBINSON	Mickele	7 MAR 1801	7 APR 1801	F	101
ROBINSON	Ralph	31 DEC 1831	24 JAN 1832	H	150
ROBINSON	Rhoda	10 AUG 1813	12 OCT 1813	G	7
ROBINSON	Thomas	26 JUL 1786	10 AUG 1787	F	82
ROBINSON	Thomas	13 AUG 1840	16 OCT 1843	K	4
RODNEY	Daniel	13 JUN 1842	5 OCT 1846	K	188
RODNEY	Ruth	5 SEP 1797	13 NOV 1806	F	259
RODNEY	Thomas	1 SEP 1817	29 MAY 1820	G	183
ROGERS	Daniel	27 JAN 1806	19 FEB 1806	F	218
ROGERS	Parker	31 AUG 1835	3 OCT 1835	H	301
ROGERS	Priscillah	3 MAY 1806	24 JUN 1806	F	237
ROSE	Charles	13 FEB 1832	8 MAY 1832	H	170

ROSE	William	23 JUL 1838	7 AUG 1838	I	137
ROSS	Caleb	5 OCT 1841	8 NOV 1841	I	298
ROSS	Clement	15 JAN 1808	30 APR 1808	F	339
ROSS	Curtis	12 DEC 1844	28 JUL 1846	K	178
ROSS	Gibson	17 MAR 1815	24 NOV 1820	G	192
ROSS	Nathaniel	17 AUG 1822	30 NOV 1822	G	269
ROSS	Robert	6 NOV 1820	21 NOV 1820	G	192
ROUSE	James	8 MAY 1820	1 JUN 1822	G	258
ROWLAND	James	25 FEB 1851	8 OCT 1851	K	573
ROWLAND	Thomas	23 SEP 1805	20 JAN 1807	F	267
RUSSEL	Emanuel	14 FEB 1810	6 OCT 1812	F	505
RUSSEL	Esther	13 JUN 1817	7 OCT 1824	G	356
RUSSEL	Frances	27 FEB 1847	4 APR 1849	K	370
RUSSELL	John	6 APR 1820	1 DEC 1823	G	308
RUST	Absolum	2 DEC 1831	23 FEB 1847	K	224
RUST	Barney	? ? ? ?	1825	G	292
RUST	John	19 OCT 1810	15 NOV 1810	F	424
RUST	John	21 JAN 1826	20 JAN 1827	G	444
RUST	William	24 AUG 1818	8 SEP 1818	G	125
SALMONS	Benjamin	JUL 1820	9 JUN 1821	G	210
SCHEY	Ferdinand	24 JAN 1841	8 DEC 1842	I	363
SCHOOLFIELD	William	14 NOV 1824	30 MAY 1826	G	424
SCOTT	Sarah	18 JUN 1847	8 JUL 1847	K	249
SEPPLE	Rachel	9 APR 1848	12 MAR 1850	K	475
SHANAHAN	Cliford	11 MAY 1808	31 AUG 1808	F	342
SHANKLAND	David	21 JUN 1809	23 FEB 1810	F	392
SHANKLAND	Sary	17 JAN 1815	27 NOV 1819	G	157
SHANKLAND	William	25 APR 1819	21 DEC 1819	G	158
SHARP	Benjamin	2 NOV 1824	11 NOV 1824	G	359
SHARP	John	13 NOV 1822	20 NOV 1822	G	266
SHARP	Joseph	2 JAN 1835	20 FEB 1840	I	216
SHAVER	John	18 SEP 1833	6 JAN 1834	H	224
SHIELDS	Eli	9 MAY 1845	8 JAN 1849	K	329
SHIRMAN	Thomas	15 FEB 1834	22 JUL 1834	H	248
SHOCKLEY	Curtis	11 APR 1831	27 SEP 1831	H	129
SHOCKLEY	Eli	19 NOV 1837	1 JUN 1843	[	393
SHOCKLEY	Elizabeth	2 APR 1842	2 APR 1846	K	155
SHOCKLEY	Karen	24 OCT 1836	13 AUG 1839	I	193
SHOCKLEY	William	21 APR 1801	28 DEC 1801	E	314
SHOCKLEY	William	9 AUG 1823	29 JUN 1824	G	335
SHORT	Ann	1 OCT 1832	9 APR 1833	H	196
SHORT	Edward	20 AUG 1802	16 MAY 1809	F	372
SHORT	Elisha	6 NOV 1810	1 DEC 1810	F	433
SHORT	Isaac	6 SEP 1824	10 JAN 1826	G	410
SHORT	Jacob	8 NOV 1805	21 NOV 1805	F	210
SHORT	John	23 DEC 1811	14 JAN 1812	F	480
SHORT	John	29 JUL 1818	25 AUG 1818	G	120
SHORT	John	24 JUL 1817	23 SEP 1831	H	126
SHORT	Ketturah	18 DEC 1843	20 MAR 1847	K	227

SHORT	Noah	30 SEP 1833	4 FEB 1834	H	227
SHORT	Noah	31 JAN 1835	13 FEB 1835	H	278
SHORT	Philip	18 DEC 1843	18 DEC 1843	K	227
SHORT	Philip	23 JAN 1844	3 JUL 1847	K	242
SHORT	Priscilla	23 JUL 1833	20 FEB 1838	I	100
SHORT	Purnal	19 FEB 1838	2 SEP 1839	I	200
SHORT	Purnal	25 SEP 1851	27 NOV 1851	K	574
SHORT	Shadrack	11 MAY 1815	6 JUN 1815	G	57
SHORT	Shadrack	5 SEP 1811	22 DEC 1823	G	313
SHORT	Wingate	23 FEB 1818	31 MAR 1818	G	114
SIMPLER	Andrew	20 APR 1841	9 MAY 1850	K	469
SIMPLER	Milby	16 DEC 1824	11 JAN 1825	G	373
SIMPLER	Thomas	16 MAR 1812	FEB 1826	G	415
SIMPLER	Thomas	? ? ? ?	29 MAY 1849	K	393
SIRMAN	Job	21 JUL 1822	13 FEB 1828	H	14
SIRMAN	John	7 JAN 1815	1 FEB 1815	G	56
SIRMAN	Lowder	7 APR 1831	8 MAY 1832	H	169
SIRMAN	William	8 AUG 1839	12 OCT 1839	I	203
SKINNER	Eleanor	14 NOV 1827	28 JAN 1828	H	8
SMITH	Alsey	24 JUL 1848	1849	K	332
SMITH	Ann	5 JAN 1807	7 APR 1807	F	275
SMITH	Cesar	21 MAR 1844	29 AUG 1848	K	316
SMITH	David	26 AUG 1831	1 OCT 1831	H	130
SMITH	David	3 JUN 1849	17 OCT 1849	K	424
SMITH	Elijah	7 NOV 1800	21 JUL 1807	F	287
SMITH	Elizabeth	APR 1835	15 AUG 1837	I	57
SMITH	George	20 JUN 1807	11 SEP 1807	F	295
SMITH	Hezekiah	1 MAY 1819	21 MAY 1819	G	144
SMITH	Hugh	14 JAN 1830	27 FEB 1832	H	159
SMITH	Job	2 JAN 1833	21 MAY 1833	H	202
SMITH	John	21 OCT 1812	15 MAY 1823	G	288
SMITH	Priscilla	10 NOV 1806	25 DEC 1806	F	246
SMITH	Sally	1 OCT 1800	24 NOV 1803	F	147
SMITH	William	7 JAN 1804	23 MAR 1804	F	145
SMITH	William	4 JUN 1845	14 JUN 1845	K	103
SMITH	William	2 FEB 1846	16 FEB 1847	K	219
SPENCER	James	19 AUG 1851	26 SEP 1851	K	553
SPICER	Betsey	7 JAN 1822	15 JAN 1822	G	231
SPICER	Curtis	17 MAY 1823	23 SEP 1823	G	296
SPICER	Elzey	7 DEC 1820	17 FEB 1821	G	198
SPICER	John	? ? ? ?	20 FEB 1849	K	337
SPICER	Lewis	18 JAN 1845	25 JAN 1845	K	72
STAFFORD	Andrew	31 DEC 1845	5 FEB 1846	K	147
STAPLEFORD	Bruffet	No Date	1830	H	93
STARR	James	30 OCT 1814	20 FEB 1815	G	54
STARR	James	18 NOV 1836	9 DEC 1836	I	13
STEEL	Ishmael	8 FEB 1812	28 DEC 1813	G	5
STEPHENSON	Kendal	19 DEC 1814	28 JAN 1815	G	42
STEVENS	William	7 AUG 1844	5 SEP 1844	K	46

STEWART	George	1 MAR 1843	5 MAR 1844	K	28
STEWART	Michael	13 APR 1812	28 MAY 1812	F	489
STOCKLEY	Elizabeth	25 OCT 1800	22 FEB 1808	F	312
STOCKLEY	George	21 APR 1801	26 APR 1801	F	60
STOCKLEY	Jacob	22 FEB 1830	18 OCT 1831	H	133
STOCKLEY	John	27 MAY 1806	3 JUL 1806	F	236
STOCKLEY	Sarah	6 APR 1823	31 MAY 1825	G	393
STOCKLEY	Woodman	7 FEB 1799	7 JAN 1800	E	302
STOCKLEY	Woodman	30 JUL 1813	15 AUG 1813	G	7
STUART	Jonathan	20 JUN 1818	7 JUL 1818	G	130
STUART	Michael	JAN 1849	22 MAR 1849	K	358
SWAIN	William	17 FEB 1811	16 MAR 1812	F	485
SWIGGETT	Nancy	10 JAN 1831	17 MAY 1831	H	108
TARR	Betsey	7 MAR 1818	1 APR 1818	G	133
TAYLOR	Dolley	15 JUL 1813	22 AUG 1814	G	38
TAYLOR	Hugh	18 APR 1813	31 MAY 1813	F	518
TAYLOR	Nancy	23 MAR 1824	3 JUN 1824	G	325
TAYLOR	Polly	20 SEP 1807	6 OCT 1807	F	296
TAYLOR	Thomas	11 JAN 1798	12 OCT 1813	G	21
TENNANT	John	15 OCT 1805	18 MAR 1806	F	221
THARP	Isaac	25 DEC 1801	11 APR 1802	F	80
THOMAS	Grace	24 NOV 1838	17 OCT 1840	I	235
THOMPSON	John	24 JAN 1808	13 FEB 1808	F	319
THOMPSON	Levin	10 OCT 1804	14 FEB 1010	C	76
THOMPSON	Littleton	9 MAR 1823	20 MAR 1823	G	285
THOMPSON	William	27 NOV 1807	15 NOV 1808	F	370
THOMPSON	William	23 NOV 1822	8 JUL 1823	G	292
THOROUGHGO	Miller	25 MAR 1824	27 APR 1824	G	324
TILNEY	Stringer	28 MAR 1826	16 MAY 1826	G	420
TIMMONS	Aaron	19 MAY 1818	1 OCT 1821	G	219
TIMMONS	Eleanor	22 SEP 1837	23 OCT 1837	I	87
TIMMONS	Mathias	20 JUN 1809	14 OCT 1809	F	420
TIMMONS	Smith	24 JUN 1838	9 APR 1839	I	176
TINDAL	Charles	15 AUG 1822	27 SEP 1831	H	128
TINDAL	Minas	23 JAN 1822	25 MAR 1822	G	244
TINDAL	Purnal	17 SEP 1831	21 APR 1832	H	167
TINDAL	Samuel	22 NOV 1816	10 DEC 1816	G	82
TINDALL	Jesse	2 MAY 1806	20 MAY 1806	F	231
TINGLE	John	27 JUL 1803	8 DEC 1807	F	326
TINGLE	Nathaniel	14 OCT 1840	20 NOV 1840	I	244
TINGLE	William	20 SEP 1806	17 FEB 1807	F	250
TINGLEY	Sarah	16 NOV 1802	12 JAN 1807	F	265
TODD	Levin	15 NOV 1812	12 APR 1814	G	4
TOWNSAND	Littleton	7 MAY 1848	7 JUL 1848	K	299
TOWNSEND	Elias	4 JAN 1821	17 JAN 1821	G	196
TOWNSEND	Jacob	19 MAR 1801	5 MAR 1803	F	110
TOWNSEND	James	4 FEB 1834	22 APR 1834	H	243
TOWNSEND	Littleton	9 SEP 1820	21 MAY 1822	G	252
TOWNSEND	Sarah	15 MAR 1813	23 JAN 1818	G	111

TOWNSEND	William	27 SEP 1794	3 JAN 1810	F	397
TOWNSEND	William	27 OCT 1816	11 OCT 1816	G	79
TRACY	James	21 DEC 1847	31 JAN 1850	K	452
TRUITT	Andrew	24 JUN 1836	26 JUL 1836	H	335
TRUITT	Betsy	4 NOV 1829	22 DEC 1829	H	57
TRUITT	Jarman	7 SEP 1822	1 OCT 1823	G	298
TRUITT	John	8 MAY 1817	22 JUL 1817	G	93
TRUITT	John	5 AUG 1818	8 DEC 1824	G	364
TRUITT	Josiah	13 JAN 1830	25 JAN 1830	H	67
TRUITT	Lankford	15 JUN 1821	20 NOV 1828	H	24
TRUITT	Mary	3 JUN 1835	8 SEP 1835	H	297
TULL	Chambers	23 DEC 1823	3 FEB 1824	G	315
TULL	Elizabeth	7 JUN 1820	11 MAR 1822	G	243
TULL	Isaac	No Date	6 JAN 1806	F	214
TULL	Jesse	No Date	13 OCT 1812	F	511
TULL	Richard	25 FEB 1797	16 FEB 1801	F	38
TUNNELL	Scarsborough	30 DEC 1807	9 FEB 1808	F	311
TWOMA	John	11 MAR 1805	15 MAR 1809	F	366
VANKIRK	George	13 JUN 1806	21 APR 1807	F	281
VANKIRK	John	14 MAR 1786	3 JUN 1805	F	195
VAUGHAN	Levin	27 MAR 1799	17 AUG 1804	F	162
VAUGHAN	William	21 APR 1835	30 NOV 1841	I	310
VENSER	Soloman	1800	7 MAR 1800	E	281
VICKARS	Nathan	9 MAR 1841	22 SEP 1841	I	289
VICKERS	Anthony	15 SEP 1810	9 OCT 1810	F	419
VICKERS	Sarah	15 APR 1801	16 JUL 1811	F	462
VINCENT	George	21 JUN 1845	28 SEP 1845	K	113
VINCENT	Joseph	23 FEB 1848	12 DEC 1848	K	325
VINSON	Benjamin	30 APR 1800	7 OCT 1800	E	267
VINSON	Benjamin	9 APR 1800	7 OCT 1800	E	271
VINSON	Elizabeth	1 JUN 1824	24 NOV 1824	G	361
VINSON	Isaac	16 JUL 1835	14 OCT 1835	H	307
VINSON	Levina	16 MAY 1814	6 JUN 1814	G	25
VINSON	Polly	9 SEP 1835	10 DEC 1835	H	310
WADKINS	John	29 DEC 1841	18 JAN 1842	I	313
WAGAMAN	Jeremiah	20 JUN 1848	29 JUL 1848	K	304
WALKER	William	5 MAR 1796	17 DEC 1800	E	269
WALLACE	James	23 MAR 1840	15 APR 1842	I	335
WALLER	Ebe	4 NOV 1845	7 JAN 1847	K	211
WALLER	Eleanor	6 JUN 1820	8 SEP 1820	G	169
WALLER	George	6 OCT 1806	10 NOV 1806	F	253
WALLER	Jonathan	18 OCT 1808	4 NOV 1808	F	346
WALLER	Thomas	9 OCT 1819	11 APR 1820	G	166
WALLS	Eli	3 JUL 1839	26 OCT 1842	I	356
WALLS	Peter	12 JUN 1846	28 MAR 1848	K	275
WALLS	Samuel	17 JAN 1833	14 MAR 1835	H	280
WALLS	Samuel	1 OCT 1843	No Date	K	24
WALLS	William	22 JAN 1797	19 NOV 1806	F	243
WALTER	John	4 MAR 1815	15 NOV 1815	G	176

WALTON	George	5 MAY 1799	19 NOV 1801	F	18
WALTON	George	7 FEB 1822	25 MAY 1829	H	44
WALTON	James	1 MAY 1848	5 SEP 1848	K	347
WALTON	Jane	12 MAR 1805	19 MAR 1808	F	323
WALTON	Jonathan	1825	3 APR 1825	G	386
WALTON	Joseph	No Date	1 NOV 1821	G	223
WALTON	Nancy	11 JAN 1845	30 JAN 1845	K	68
WALTON	Polly	28 NOV 1822	7 JAN 1823	G	275
WAPLES	Gidion	15 JUN 1837	26 SEP 1837	I	66
WAPLES	Joseph	3 JUN 1825	OCT 1825	G	399
WAPLES	Mary	25 APR 1839	27 FEB 1843	I	372
WAPLES	Paul	13 JUN 1800	9 JAN 1801	F	5
WAPLES	Rhoda	5 APR 1828	24 JUN 1828	H	19
WAPLES	Thomas	NOV 1850	17 DEC 1850	K	501
WAPLES	Wallace	10 JUN 1837	20 MAR 1838	I	111
WAPLES	William	1 FEB 1802	20 FEB 1810	F	389
WAPLES	William	30 NOV 1811	21 FEB 1812	F	488
WAPLES	William	17 JUL 1841	5 NOV 1841	I	295
WARD	Mary	14 FEB 1848	23 JUL 1850	K	480
WARD	Moses	25 JUL 1811	17 SEP 1813	F	521
WARD	Murphy	7 JUL 1812	2 MAR 1813	G	11
WARD	Thomas	15 NOV 1832	17 JAN 1837	I	22
WARE	John	10 MAR 1827	29 MAY 1827	G	454
WARREN	Alexander	14 APR 1809	25 APR 1809	F	369
WARREN	Bennet	7 MAR 1833	19 MAR 1833	H	192
WARREN	Boaz	7 NOV 1850	22 NOV 1850	K	497
WARREN	Boaze	13 APR 1837	14 AUG 1849	K	410
WARREN	Ebenezar	14 MAR 1813	3 MAY 1816	G	78
WARREN	Levi	10 APR 1799	17 NOV 1801	E	293
WARREN	Lodawick	31 MAR 1848	20 APR 1848	K	281
WARREN	Major	6 MAR 1849	7 OCT 1851	K	563
WARREN	Sinah	1 MAY 1826	17 APR 1827	G	451
WARREN	Spicer	21 NOV 1846	8 DEC 1846	K	205
WARREN	Stephen	22 SEP 1846	7 OCT 1846	K	190
WARRENTON	Luke	15 MAR 1815	12 JAN 1821	G	185
WARRINGTON	Alexander	19 JAN 1847	5 OCT 1847	K	256
WARRINGTON	Anna	28 JAN 1832	23 APR 1836	H	326
WARRINGTON	Hester	27 JUN 1815	3 SEP 1816	G	179
WARRINGTON	James	6 DEC 1838	2 APR 1846	K	152
WARRINGTON	Joseph	4 NOV 1824	24 DEC 1829	H	58
WARRINGTON	Luke	3 JAN 1811	18 MAY 1813	F	519
WARRINGTON	Sarah	8 DEC 1806	24 FEB 1807	F	258
WARRINGTON	Stephen	2 APR 1823	21 APR 1823	G	286
WATSON	Beniah	21 OCT 1844	6 NOV 1844	K	55
WATSON	Beniah	? ? ? ?	1850	K	472
WATSON	Paynter	21 JUN 1851	22 JUL 1851	K	540
WATSON	Philip	21 JAN 1850	18 JUN 1850	K	479
WATSON	Smothers	13 FEB 1817	10 MAY 1817	G	113
WATTSON	Robert	13 FEB 1811	21 MAR 1815	G	54

26

WEB	Benjamin	AUG 1803	20 MAR 1804	F	128
WEBB	Dorman	15 NOV 1802	29 JAN 1803	F	44
WEBB	Esther	18 NOV 1828	29 DEC 1828	H	28
WEBB	Jacob	5 DEC 1805	24 SEP 1806	F	239
WEBB	James	7 NOV 1822	30 NOV 1822	G	270
WEST	Arthur	16 AUG 1831	15 NOV 1831	H	139
WEST	Jacob	28 FEB 1803	18 MAY 1804	F	137
WEST	James	18 NOV 1820	20 AUG 1829	H	48
WEST	John	9 APR 1806	23 FEB 1808	F	329
WEST	John	25 MAY 1832	17 OCT 1836	I	4
WEST	John	12 MAR 1845	18 APR 1845	K	95
WEST	Kendal	17 NOV 1822	28 MAR 1823	G	283
WEST	Lemuel	8 AUG 1812	21 JAN 1813	G	9
WEST	Nancy	18 NOV 1820	20 AUG 1829	H	48
WEST	Phillip	7 OCT 1840	16 APR 1841	I	264
WEST	Robert	7 NOV 1809	22 FEB 1810	F	395
WEST	Thomas	22 DEC 1800	18 APR 1802	E	318
WEST	Thomas	15 OCT 1845	25 NOV 1845	K	131
WEST	WIlliam	23 DEC 1800	29 JUL 1801	F	61
WHARTON	Denaris	1 OCT 1810	15 OCT 1810	F	417
WHARTON	Henman	29 MAR 1800	7 JAN 1801	E	290
WHARTON	Matthew	18 JAN 1802	9 FEB 1802	E	301
WHITE	Eli	21 NOV 1803	4 MAR 1805	F	181
WHITE	James	5 APR 1833	5 FEB 1834	H	230
WHITE	William	24 MAR 1804	10 MAY 1811	F	458
WILDGOOSE	Jenny	21 NOV 1802	15 DEC 1802	E	313
WILDY	Charles	13 NOV 1804	9 MAY 1806	F	229
WILEY	Samuel	3 FEB 1849	2 APR 1849	K	368
WILKINS	James	6 NOV 1807	16 JUL 1808	F	441
WILKINS	Ruth	17 DEC 1804	19 JAN 1805	F	174
WILLEY	Marget	3 JAN 1816	12 AUG 1816	G	28
WILLEY	Nathan	10 JAN 1812	18 JAN 1812	F	490
WILLEY	Solomon	28 JAN 1816	10 DEC 1816	G	85
WILLIAM	Edward	31 JUL 1824	14 DEC 1824	G	366
WILLIAMS	Amelia	13 NOV 1812	1 DEC 1812	F	514
WILLIAMS	Arthur	22 SEP 1828	11 MAR 1829	H	38
WILLIAMS	Charles	29 JAN 1818	1 MAY 1818	G	129
WILLIAMS	Ezekial	1 MAR 1834	13 SEP 1836	H	339
WILLIAMS	Ezekial	SEP 1846	19 OCT 1846	K	199
WILLIAMS	Isabella	17 JUL 1839	17 AUG 1839	I	198
WILLIAMS	James	11 APR 1851	2 SEP 1851	K	551
WILLIAMS	Jesse	15 JUN 1805	25 JUN 1805	F	197
WILLIAMS	Job	9 JUN 1806	3 JUL 1807	F	289
WILLIAMS	John	18 SEP 1803	23 NOV 1803	F	151
WILLIAMS	John	23 OCT 1807	2 NOV 1810	F	429
WILLIAMS	John	4 FEB 1816	16 FEB 1816	G	65
WILLIAMS	Levin	27 JUL 1834	23 AUG 1834	H	253
WILLIAMS	Mooder	20 APR 1822	9 JUL 1822	G	258
WILLIAMS	Nathan	29 MAR 1826	20 FEB 1830	H	71

WILLIAMS	Pheby	6 FEB 1836	2 NOV 1843	K	15
WILLIAMS	Pricilla	29 MAR 1823	22 MAR 1825	G	384
WILLIAMS	Samuel	1 APR 1818	5 JUL 1822	G	238
WILLIAMS	Whittington	17 MAR 1807	7 APR 1807	F	276
WILLIAMS	William	29 JAN 1828	25 MAR 1828	H	15
WILLISS	John	2 NOV 1817	11 MAR 1819	G	139
WILLS	William	10 SEP 1827	24 MAR 1829	H	39
WILSON	David	14 JAN 1841	10 FEB 1842	I	315
WILSON	Elizabeth	27 SEP 1848	4 SEP 1849	K	415
WILSON	John	1825	29 DEC 1825	G	408
WILSON	Joshua	7 SEP 1809	13 FEB 1810	F	387
WILSON	Samuel	3 APR 1846	13 NOV 1849	K	448
WILSON	Sarah	23 JAN 1823	2 MAR 1823	G	279
WILSON	Simon	21 NOV 1839	No Date	I	210
WILSON	Thomas	1 AUG 1795	17 JAN 1806	F	216
WILSON	Thomas	27 AUG 1817	8 SEP 1817	G	108
WILSON	Thomas	10 NOV 1851	2 DEC 1851	K	577
WILSON	William	1 JUL 1800	15 JUN 1807	F	284
WILSON	William	6 SEP 1845	14 OCT 1845	K	119
WILTBANK	Cornelius	27 MAY 1813	23 NOV 1813	G	14
WILTBANK	Rachel	21 MAR 1804	13 SEP 1808	F	343
WINDSOR	James	26 FEB 1800	26 AUG 1806	F	264
WINGATE	John	5 DEC 1817	22 SEP 1818	G	119
WINGATE	John	15 JUN 1818	19 DEC 1821	G	220
WINGATE	Thomas	28 MAR 1836	14 APR 1836	H	324
WINWRIGHT	Levin	9 FEB 1814	8 MAR 1814	G	35
WINWRIGHT	William	17 JAN 1814	1 FEB 1814	G	39
WISE	George	6 MAY 1826	8 MAY 1827	G	453
WITTGOOS	Robert	2 FEB 1828	22 SEP 1829	H	51
WOLFE	Daniel	18 JUN 1823	18 JUN 1824	G	329
WOLFE	William	4 JUL 1818	11 JUL 1818	G	116
WOOTTEN	John	13 JUL 1830	2 AUG 1848	K	306
WOOTTEN	William	14 MAR 1839	15 AUG 1839	I	195
WORKMAN	Bridget	31 DEC 1835	19 JAN 1836	H	313
WORKMAN	John	2 APR 1843	10 MAY 1843	I	386
WRIGHT	Isaac	APR 1848	16 FEB 1850	K	466
WRIGHT	Jacob	17 APR 1818	18 MAY 1818	G	87
WRIGHT	Jesse	1 APR 1808	26 AUG 1808	F	436
WRIGHT	John	8 DEC 1825	19 DEC 1825	G	405
WRIGHT	Joshua	1 MAY 1814	10 JUN 1814	G	36
WRIGHT	Sally	15 MAR 1830	11 OCT 1830	H	95
WYATT	Jane	10 JAN 1830	18 JAN 1832	H	147
WYATT	Sacker	14 AUG 1800	30 SEP 1800	F	49
WYATT	William	21 APR 1806	3 MAR 1807	F	268
YANCEY	Henry	4 MAR 1809	1825	G	385
YOUNG	Nathan	26 DEC 1818	14 JAN 1819	G	135
YOUNG	Nathaniel	16 FEB 1803	12 JUN 1804	F	132

www.ingramcontent.com/pod-product-compliance
Lightning Source LLC
Chambersburg PA
CBHW060553030426
42337CB00019B/3541